Cover map courtesy of U.S. Geological Survey,
Menlo Park, California

1919 *Stavangerfjord* travel poster on p. 34
courtesy of Norwegian America Lines, Oslo

Several of the stories in *Captain Hardscratch and Others* appeared in
the 1993 *Pilothouse Guide* of the *Alaska Fisherman's Journal*, Seattle

Printed in the United States of America
First printed August 1993
Hardscratch Press, Walnut Creek, California

Library of Congress Card Number: 92-76133

ISBN: 0-9625429-6-2

1 2 3 4 5 6 7 8 9 0

Alaska
Journey
1919-1934

An adventurous young
Norwegian's coming-of-age

By Ralph Soberg

A HARDSCRATCH PRESS BOOK

"I was 18 years old
and green as a hick can be,
but full of self-confidence."

(Confessions of an Alaska Bootlegger,
Chapter 1)

Editor's Note

Ralph Soberg's first book, *Survival on Montague Island,* was written and published in his 83d year. In the next two years came three more books about his adventurous life: *Confessions of an Alaska Bootlegger, Bridging Alaska/From the Big Delta to the Kenai,* and—going back to his roots in Norway—*Captain Hardscratch and Others.* At the time of his death at age 85, in December 1992, he was working on material for this compiled volume. *Alaska Journey 1919-1934* contains in chronological order *Captain Hardscratch, Montague Island* and *Bootlegger.* It carries his story to the start of a 30-year career with the Alaska Road Commission and the opening of *Bridging Alaska.*

Always conscious of his lack of formal education, Ralph Soberg resisted being called an author. He was a constant, appreciative reader, and for him "author" was reserved for James Michener and John Steinbeck and other favorites. But that honest deference aside, he took frank delight in the responses to his own books. Reviewers praised his "light touch and easy humor" and called him "a true storyteller," and he heard from readers young and old—Alaskans and former Alaskans (if there is such a thing) and people who hoped one day to visit Alaska, as well as those who simply had a keen interest in the kind of unvarnished personal history he narrated.

A pinnacle of one sort was reached the day an appreciative piece about Ralph Soberg and his books appeared in the *Seattle Post-Intelligencer* (Nov. 30, 1991). "I never thought I'd see myself in the newspaper next to Ann Landers!" was his wide-eyed reaction—never mind columnist Jon Hahn's carefully crafted prose. (It was Jon Hahn who first encouraged the writing of *Captain Hardscratch and Others,* and he wrote the delightful foreword to it, which appears again in this volume.)

Another source of pleasure was the frequent phone contact with such readers as the daughter of a 1920s law enforcement official who, according to the author in *Confessions of an Alaska Bootlegger,* "still owes me for two gallons of good moonshine." She was cheerfully absolved of her father's debt.

But the most dramatic consequence of the books came in the fall of

1992, a few months before Ralph Soberg's death, when he was reunited with his stepdaughter Daphne Doreen Phillips after a separation of almost 50 years. She had happened across his first two books and located him by telephone, then traveled to visit him in Ballard. Generally a frontier egalitarian—"Don't ever let anyone tell you a woman can't be a great mechanic!" he exclaimed one day to a startled visitor—but also possessed of his own strong sense of propriety, he had not mentioned his early, unhappy marriage in any of the books. But Daphne has a place in them, particularly *Bridging Alaska,* and everyone concerned is grateful for the timing of that reunion.

People have asked how these accounts of long-ago happenings came to be. "Did he keep a diary?" is a frequent question, and the answer is no. The stories had always been there; the storyteller had to be nudged only a little to set them down. Occasional details were checked against the orderly confusion of "old maps, navigational charts and photographs" that Jon Hahn described in his column, and old friends were usually willing partners in the process of recollection and research.

As Ralph Soberg's daughter as well as his editor, I say "usually" with a smile that those other associates would understand. In *Bridging Alaska,* he acknowledges that he could be a relentless taskmaster. Quick-witted and keen-minded to the very end, he was not always patient with more plodding mortals, especially when there was a job he had decided must be done. Overnight mail was invented for him. "Hi, honey," he would say to his editor by long-distance telephone. "I found some more pictures. I'll send them this afternoon." The next day, another call: "Well?"

But he was greatly moved by the encouragement as well as the occasional footwork of friends and acquaintances, and he took pains to express his gratitude in the books. Joanne Jeppeson, who typed all the original drafts from his Norwegian-accented tapes and rough manuscripts, was high on the list. Fellow writers Martin Cole and Margaret Q. Breedman were singled out for their early support, as were such people as George Baker (who combed through old newspaper files for stories on the Slippery Four), Kay Boyd, Robert De Armond, youngest daughter Jerry Fallon, cousin Rønnaug Pedersen Johnson, Virginia Newton, son-in-law Werner Pels, and the late Ben Stewart, mentor and lifelong friend, and his brother Judge Tom Stewart.

Ralph and Daphne Doreen at Takotna, about 1940

Alaska journalist George Sundborg wrote a foreword to Confessions of an Alaska Bootlegger that deftly puts the story in perspective. Illustrator John Boring spent hours with the author going over the details that make the maps such an important part of the books. And without designer David Johnson there would be no books. It was he and Ralph who convinced me that the adventure on Montague Island could stand on its own. From that small start came Hardscratch Press, and we all have been proud of the results.

Each of the original books included here carries its own dedication. Honoring his partner of 45 years, *Survival on Montague Island* begins simply "to Ruth, a true Alaskan." *Confessions of an Alaska Bootlegger* was dedicated "to the memory of Charlie Sinclair, George 'Rocky' Johnsen, and Sam Elstead, my three dependable and honest partners, always cool under pressure." *Captain Hardscratch and Others* is "for my father and mother." But it was Ralph Soberg's expressed intention that this volume, his last book, be dedicated to Norman Lauritzen, whose good heart and good humor and unstinting friendship were beacons at the close of the journey.

> Jackie Pels
> Walnut Creek, California
> April 21, 1993

As he instructed, Ralph Soberg's ashes will be buried this spring at the gravesite of his father, John Edvard Johannessen, overlooking Hardscratch Point on Unga Island.

[Captain Hardscratch *and* Others]

1.
Captain Nikolai 17

2.
Norway 21

3.
To the New World 35

4.
Unga Island 47

Foreword

Ralph Soberg was born in a manger—literally—and raised—again, literally—on a rock. He spent much of his young life raising hell.

That life moderated somewhat, if only because there's just so much hell-raising you could get away with in a strict Norwegian farming-and-fishing family.

This isn't about ringing doorbells on the way home from Luther League meetings somewhere in Minnesota. This is one heckuva lot of hard work and hard living over 85 years and God-only-knows how many miles of open ocean and barren rock and tundra and snow.

When Ralph's family moved from a tiny village 200 miles north of the Arctic Circle to what was supposed to be a better life in the New World, you'd have thought they might pick something more comfortable or more promising than a huge rock in Alaska's Shumagin Islands, at the head of the Aleutian chain. It reads almost too far away and too long ago to be in any time zone, but it has all happened in his lifetime.

Not surprising that they called their rocky farm and *stokkfisk* station "Hardscratch." And after 85 years of doing everything from hardhat diving and bootlegging to bridge-building, it's not surprising that Soberg can build a book from scratch.

What is surprising is that after three earlier, well-built books about his work and life, he still has a lot of wonderful stories to tell. These are the stories I knew were just under the surface of the earlier books, stories about parents and siblings and neighbors and other pioneers—and they were that in every sense—carving a subsistence and a future out of hard times and hard places.

Captain Hardscratch and Others is not a slick, cleverly woven literary production. It's built more like a stone *uthus*, with the heavy, earthy smell of hay and animals, the tang of salt air and fish, and the breeziness of uncomplicated story-telling.

I wrinkled my nose imagining what Uncle Nick's fishing boat, Baby #2, smelled like with its diesel engine running on homemade cod liver oil.

Hardscratch in the 1920s

And anyone would shudder at what One-Eyed Lena did with a cat, to a man. Uff Da! In between, there are some very warm, funny, touching scenes: innocent naked boys walking down their first-ever hotel hallway to the bath, a young man and his mother doing farm chores, a father tearfully embracing two of his sons in a fishing dory as the young men leave Hardscratch forever.

Captain Hardscratch holds the sort of dauntless spirit that makes stories worth telling and life worth living.

Jon Hahn
Seattle
April 16, 1992

Jon Hahn has been a columnist for the *Seattle Post-Intelligencer* since 1981, and a newspaper reporter, on and off, since 1962, including 10 years for the former *Chicago Daily News*. He has a master's degree (journalism) in the bottom of his sock drawer and a not-so-hidden admiration for anything built-from-scratch, home-spun or home-cooked. His father was a tin-bender and his great-grandfather was one of Chicago's last blacksmiths. His grandfather came from the same town in Germany as his wife's grandfather. Judith, an artist, and Jon have been married almost 30 years and have one son. Jon has written one book, *Legally Sane,* a nonfiction account of a serial killer. It went on remainders (Regnery & Co.) almost immediately.

1.

Captain Nikolai

Hardscratch—properly named!

We landed there from Norway in mid-August 1919, Mother, Dad, my three brothers and I.

Mother and Dad were worn out after nearly three months of travel with four lively boys. The youngest, Egil, was only 6 years old. Eivind (Ed) was 14, Birger, who became Fred with the move from Norway, was 13, and I was 11, almost 12.

Our sister, Ida Elisabet, had had to stay behind in Norway because she had tuberculosis of the bone in her left leg. Two years later she passed immigration and came over by herself. She was two years younger than I.

Dad, the only one of us who spoke any English, had been in the Klondike Gold Rush in 1898 with my Uncle Nick Johannessen. They

Uncle Nikolai Johannessen ("Captain Hardscratch")

17

had no luck in four years of prospecting, and Dad had gone back home to Søberg, in the Vesterålen off the northern coast of Norway, to take over the family farm and care for his parents. My mother, Jørgine Eriksen Eikemo, had been helping on the farm while he was in America. When he returned, they got smitten and soon married and proceeded to raise a family. Mother was 20 when they married, 14 years younger than Dad. Her family lived in Stokmarknes, about 50 miles from Søberg.

Dad's parents, Johan Johannessen and Elen Maria Matiasdatter Mørk, had had two daughters, Helene and Nikoline, who married and moved away before I was born. Then came four sons, Nikolai, Kristian, Ole and John, my father.

Nikolai Johannessen, a self-taught navigator, sailed the world and became a ship's captain. Kristian Søberg was a telegrapher and Ole Søberg a well-known photographer and woodcarver. Besides supporting his family as a fisherman, John Johannessen, my dad, taught himself music and traveled throughout Norway as director of a men's choral group.

Søberg means "mountain by the sea." (The slash across the "o" gives it an "ew" sound.) *Sjø* is sea, *berg* is mountain. My brother Fred and I both chose the name Soberg when we applied for U.S. citizenship—by then Alaska was full of Johannessens of one spelling or another.

Captain Nick, later to be known as Captain Hardscratch, was in Seattle in 1898 when he heard about the gold strike in Alaska. He wrote to his youngest brother, and Dad, who of course was single at the time, joined him in the Klondike. Like so many others, however, they found only gravel.

When Dad went back to Norway from the Klondike, Uncle Nick floated down the Yukon River on a makeshift boat to Nome, where again he was too late to strike it rich. By this time, gold seekers were piling up in Dutch Harbor and Unalaska in the Aleutians because the ships that brought them from San Francisco had too

18

much draft and could not get close enough to Nome.

Nick chartered a small schooner and hauled the hopeful prospectors from Unalaska to Nome until it, like the other gold fields, petered out. Then he went to San Francisco and had a small schooner of his own built, which he named the Edna Watts after a lost sweetheart. He returned to the Aleutians and led a crew of Aleuts who hunted sea otter with spears.

By 1915, the U.S. government had outlawed the killing of sea otters to preserve the species from extermination, and Captain Nick sailed around the islands looking for a place to build a codfish station to put up salt salmon and *stokkfisk*—dried cod—for lutefisk.

He wound up in the village of Unga on Unga Island in the Shumagins, at the head of the Aleutian chain. Being a shipwright and carpenter—a good one, too, I might add—he built houses and some huge cyanide tanks for the Unga gold mine that was then in operation. Finally, in a cove north of Squaw Harbor, he constructed a permanent fish station and called it Hardscratch.

The name eventually was adopted on the nautical charts as Hardscratch Point, and thus he earned his nickname.

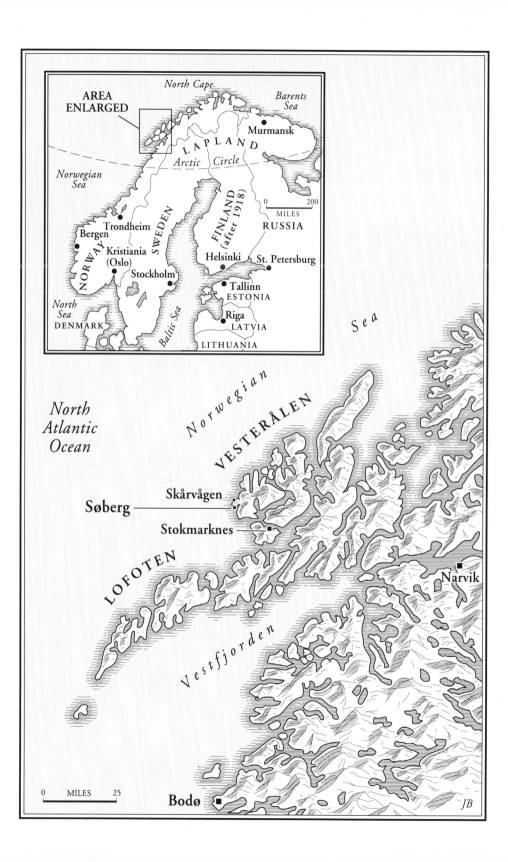

AREA
ENLARGED

North Cape

Barents
Sea

Murmansk

L A P L A N D

Arctic Circle

Norwegian
Sea

FINLAND
(after 1918)

0   200
MILES

RUSSIA

Trondheim

Bergen

Kristiania
(Oslo)

Helsinki

St. Petersburg

NORWAY

SWEDEN

Stockholm

Tallinn
ESTONIA

North
Sea

DENMARK

Baltic Sea

Riga

LATVIA

LITHUANIA

North
Atlantic
Ocean

Norwegian

VESTERÅLEN

Sea

Skårvågen

Søberg

Stokmarknes

Narvik

LOFOTEN

Vestfjorden

0   MILES   25

Bodø

JB

2.

Norway

Back in Søberg, having heard from his brother of the possibilities at Hardscratch, Dad applied for permission for us to emigrate to the United States. But war was declared on Germany, and we had to wait until 1919.

Life was never easy in our village 200 miles north of the Arctic Circle, but the German blockade during World War I meant new hardships and shortages. Fruits of any kind were unavailable, but boatloads of cabbage and kolhrabi—ugh!—came through from Denmark some way. I hated that with all my heart. We did have lots of homegrown food: potatoes and turnips (never was too fond of them, either) and, of course, lutefisk. Learning to be satisfied with what we had probably helped prepare Fred and me for being marooned on Montague Island a few years later.

There was no refrigeration, but some foods kept all winter without

My parents, Jørgine Eriksen Eikemo and John Edvard Johannessen

21

spoiling—blood pudding and sausages, head cheese and such. Mother made *flatbrød* on a large griddle, about 15 inches wide, that hung over the fireplace. After it was baked it was stacked upstairs for winter.

Our homegrown potatoes were washed and dried and sorted and put into bins in the cellar. The little ones were kept in a special bin for seed in the spring.

Coffee came in green beans that we roasted at home. I remember well having to grind them every day in a hand grinder. Coffee was used sparingly. Mother added chicory to make it darker.

We bought hard sugar in a large cone about 10 inches high. A small hatchet just for that purpose was used to break off chunks, then a pair of hand cutters was used to cut the sugar into lumps for coffee. During the blockade, just imagine: no lump sugar! For good Norwegian coffee-drinkers, a near catastrophe. As a substitute, when we could get it, granulated sugar was spread with a little water in a shallow pan and baked, then scored in small squares before it hardened.

Always, in the fall it was butchering time.

As the calves, pigs and lambs not needed for next year were slaughtered, we kids had to help save all the blood we could. Dad either shot or knocked the animals in the head. Then, laying an animal on its side, he cut the jugular vein, and we kept a dishpan under the throat so we could catch the blood. We whipped it with a special implement to keep it from coagulating.

The blood was used to make puddings and sausages to be kept in the *stabbur*, a separate storeroom on pillars at the corner of the house, with lots of vents, well-aerated from the outside.

Nothing from the butchered animals was thrown away. Tallow for soap and lubricants was made from the guts and other parts, and the head was used for sausages and head cheese, a jellied loaf made with scraps of meat.

Manure from the cows we kept was mixed with the hay used on the barn floor (to keep the floor dry) and put into a compost pile for fertilizer in spring.

The village of Søberg (background)—taken on a trip
my brother Fred and I made in 1974

Peat was our main source of fuel for heating and cooking. In the fall before too much frost, we first cut out fresh patches of topsoil, with moss and grasses still on. These we stacked in domino-like order to dry in an area to one side. Then came the black, wet bottom soil, the peat. The deeper we went, the better the peat. We cut it into squares of about 8″ × 8″ × 12″ deep. When the water had drained off, we sliced each square like a loaf of bread into 2-inch slices and stacked them, also, then left both the loam and the peat to dry until the first snow.

Then we rushed and piled them into high, round stacks to be swept clear of snow as needed and hauled home on a sled during the winter. The slices of loam, with hay and dried moss in them, were used to start the fires.

We were visited each year by bands of Laplanders and their reindeer herds. Lapland lies across Finland, Sweden and Norway. In early spring, the Lapps would travel across the three countries to the water's edge. There the herds swam to the islands off Norway's coast for the calving season. In late summer, they headed back toward the east, and Mother, with our help, would hurry to pick the cranberries from our peat property before the reindeer's broad hooves could trample the berry patches.

The Lapps, a short, Mongolian people, were wonderful to see

Dad (center, light suit) and his choir. Reinholdt Pedersen, father of my cousin, Rønnaug Pedersen Johnson, who gave me this photo, is in the upper left corner

in their brightly embroidered summer parkas and footgear with long pointed toes. The reindeer harnesses were hung with bells that announced their arrival.

Our house in Søberg was actually a sort of duplex. One end was used as a workplace, and Dad's choir practiced there.

Our whole family was taught to make music, and sometimes we sang with the choir. As we grew up, Ed was the tenor, I the bass, Birger (Fred) in-between, and Mother and Sister sang, too. Dad could organize a group of singers on almost a moment's notice. He always had a tuning fork handy. He himself played flute and wrote music. Ed and I played at playing the guitar, and Birger played the violin.

Dad's choir sang hymns and folksongs in addition to some of the songs he wrote. I remember especially liking one of the folksongs, "Pål sine høner" ("Paul's Chickens").

Mother had a spinning wheel to make yarn, and a large loom for weaving cloth. The loom was terribly intricate. It took a month to set up, with two sets of dozens and dozens of linen threads up and down hooked to a foot treadle that switched them back and forth. We helped feed raked wool sheared from our sheep to Mother when she was spinning yarn. With the finished cloth, she made clothes for us all on her sewing machine. We boys wore short trousers that covered the knee, with socks that Mother knit.

Dad made our leather shoes and also made or repaired shoes for half the people in Søberg, as well as making shoes with ice creepers for the horses in wintertime. *Luggan,* our winter footwear, similar to Alaskan mukluks, came to above the knee with a last inside and were made of cloth with heavily stitched soles. Much of the time we wore *kloggan*—wooden clogs—which we slipped off at the door.

We were able to swim all summer long in Søberg. The Gulf Stream from Mexico, which swings north past Iceland and hits near

Our swimming beach at Søberg, 1974

North Cape, Norway, before heading back out into the North Atlantic and meeting the North Sea, keeps that part of Norway ice-free and warmer than southern Norway.

I decided when I was 6 or 7 that it was time for me to learn to swim in the ocean. I sneaked off and "borrowed" a *lettbåt*—that's a light boat—at Skårvågen and rowed around the harbor to our swimming beach about three miles west of Søberg. I undressed and left my clothes on shore. Then I rowed out to about 10 feet of water and dropped the painter overboard with a rock on it.

I had never before gone beyond where my toes could reach the bottom, but I decided it was now or never. I gave it a little thought and decided to jump over the bow where I would be close to the

26

rope, so that if I couldn't dog-paddle to shore, I could grab it and get back on board again. But I made it. In my mind, I was crossing the Atlantic all by myself.

Questions were soon asked about the boat, which I had left out there, and I had to confess. Mother was upset, but I had the feeling she was proud of me, too.

My mother was just the best. I think I gave her a hard time from beginning to end. She used to shake her head and say, "I wonder what will happen to you before you leave this world."

One incident in particular I think had something to do with shaping my life, both good and bad.

I was 7 or 8 and had a bad toothache. Mother told Birger to take me to the office of the veterinarian—the horse doctor—to see if he could do something for me.

The doctor felt of my teeth and located a bad lower molar. He grabbed a pair of ugly-looking pliers, got hold of the tooth, gripped my neck and head in a strong hold like a vise, and wiggled the tooth, then broke it loose. I was pretty strong and agile—I used to lick my brothers, who were two and three years older—but he won. Out came the tooth.

I yelled bloody murder. I scared the hell out of my brother and the doctor, and spit blood all over the doctor's face and white jacket.

The doctor said to Birger, "Take this wild Indian home and tell your mother never to send him back to me again. Tell her he bellowed like a bull."

We walked home the couple of miles, and by that time the bleeding had pretty well stopped. When Mother heard what had happened, she smiled and said, "What can you expect? He was born in a barn, just like the young bulls."

Birger, of course, used this later whenever he was angry at me, calling me a pig or a cow, and the other kids in school found out and used it, too. This made me so mad I would fight anybody, no matter how big. Finally the teacher felt sorry for me, which didn't help. Now the kids called me teacher's pet, and that added fuel to the fire.

I really was born in the barn. Mother often told people, to my embarrassment, that Jesus had nothing on me, that I, too, was born in a manger. She told of sitting down on the oak stool to milk a cow and then realizing that I was on my way. She sent Eivind, then 3 years old, running to a neighbor for help, while she managed to put me in some hay in the cow's feed bin.

Dad was out fishing in the Lofotens, of course, like they always were, and the barn animals had to be cared for. She was the greatest.

(That same veterinarian visited all the little farms like ours in the fall and castrated animals we wanted to keep over the winter. The year he pulled my tooth I would gladly have done that to him, believe me!)

I had a close friend in Søberg named Frederik. What I didn't think of, he did. We wanted to be tough, so we would fight until we had bloody noses. But we never were very angry with each other, at least not for long. We were not bad boys, really, but not good, either.

My family had a tomcat with a habit of squirting urine on whatever was hanging on our clothesline. Frederik and I, both about 6 at the time, took it upon ourselves to cure the smelly problem. We had heard that a cat had nine lives and figured that if we ended this one, our cat might be a better pet in his next life. (Please remember, you animal lovers, that we too loved our cats, dogs, sheep and their lambs, and piglets, even though we sometimes had to help butcher them. In our defense, we were used to seeing dead animals, and this one certainly was nothing but trouble, fighting with the other toms to have all the females to himself, and making our clothes unwearable.)

Our first solution didn't work: a rope with a knot slipped over the cat's head and pulled tight, Frederik on one end of the rope and

Mother's parents at Stokmarknes

me on the other. One end was too short, and the cat in its mad gyrations managed to reach Frederik's hand with its claws and hang on for dear life. Frederik, of course, had to let go of the rope and get the cat off his bloody hand.

We didn't give up, though. We managed to get the cat into a gunny sack along with some rocks and proceeded to our swimming beach, where we dropped the sack into deep water and watched it go down. The poor cat was still fighting for its life. It went 'round and 'round. I can still see it go down—and I remember well the tanning we got from Mother and Dad afterward. It still burns. Also, we learned that the story about the nine lives wasn't true.

Except for the teasing—"Born in the barn! Born in the barn!"—I liked school. Children from Søberg and Skårvågen studied in a small two-room building in Søberg, the first through fifth grades in

Uncle Peter, one of Mother's brothers, with his wife, my Aunt Anna, at Stokmarknes

one room, everyone else in the other. I had just begun to understand fractions when we left Norway.

We and our neighbors had fences of wire strung on wood posts to keep the barn animals contained. In the fall, when the haying was in full process, the hay was raked and hung on the two rows of wire to dry, making a kind of hedge between the yards.

One of our neighbors was a blacksmith who was not much liked, especially by us boys. Many times we saw him kick the horses he was shoeing, and he was known to be unkind to his wife. He was a bit deaf, which helped us play tricks on him, but he could run like the devil, so when he would catch us maybe depositing a cow pie on his doorstep, he would give us a good spanking—which of course didn't add to our affection for him.

30

Mother sent me to the blacksmith's house one day to borrow half a cup of sugar. That's the way we got along up there. We borrowed from each other, all the neighbors in Søberg, just like Alaskans out in the bush.

I got over there and knocked on the door, and he, with his gruff voice, said, *"Kom inn."* I walked in slowly, cautiously. I was scared of the man. When I got inside the door, he turned around from the table, where he was sitting on a bench with one end pulled out from the wall, glared at me and said, "Speak your errand and go home."

The Mrs. asked me nicely what I wanted and then brought me the sugar, and I got the devil out of there, I can tell you. But before I left, she said to him, pointing at the bench coming from the wall at a right angle, "Where will I sit then?"

"You can sit on the floor," he said. I still remember my shock at that. "But how will I reach the food?" she said, maybe trying to make a joke of it. *"Klor etter det,"* he said harshly—"Claw for it." That's the kind of man he was.

Our Dad, who like Mother had a down-to-earth sense of humor, gave us boys an idea one day for a harmless practical joke to play on our unfriendly neighbor.

We knew from perpetually keeping an eye on him that the blacksmith used to visit the fence to do his bowel movements at a certain time of the evening, rather than use the outhouse in the barn.

Eivind, Birger and I waited on our side of the fence one moonlit evening for him to make his nightly visit. He crouched down to perform his duty, and we slipped the barn shovel under him. When he was finished, he used some hay from the hedge for toilet paper. Then, as one will do, he turned around to admire what he had done—but there was nothing there. We had pulled the shovel with his deposit on it back under the fence. With a look on his face that had us trying hard not to laugh out loud, he pulled up his pants quickly and ran for his house. He just knew he had done something, but . . .

The next day, Dad gave us each a piece of candy for a job well done.

Some days later, my pal Frederik and I walked past where the blacksmith was working his big forge with a long piece of steel on the anvil. When he saw us coming, he rested one end of the steel bar on the ground and put his free hand on his hip, studying us as we went by grunting loudly with every step.

"I know you've been up to no good," he said at last. "If I could catch you at it, I would ram this rod down your gullet until it came out the other end." We took off running like the devil was after us.

Norwegian America Line

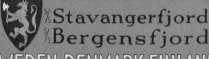

Twin-Screw Mail and
Passenger Service

S/S Stavangerfjord
S/S Bergensfjord

NEW YORK·NORWAY·SWEDEN·DENMARK·FINLAND

AND OTHER EUROPEAN COUNTRIES

3.

To the New World

On the 16th of May 1919, we were finally on our way to America and Hardscratch. I remember it well; it was the day before Norwegian Constitution Day.

We walked in single file down to the boat landing. We had to cross the fjord there to go to where the steamer would pick us up.

There was Dad, Mother, Eivind, Birger, me, Ida and Egil, all in rotation, the little ones last. All of Søberg was standing there at the landing to shake hands with us. Everyone was crying and wishing us well but the blacksmith. (I've had plenty of time to think that he may have been OK in many ways. After all, we were not angels.)

A long, difficult voyage lay ahead. Three months! I don't know how Mother and Dad stood it.

Cousin Rønnaug and her family left Norway nine years after we did, traveling on the *Bergensfjord*—sister ship to the *Stavangerfjord*—to Halifax and then on to Seattle, where she is now our next-door neighbor

First time Birger and I got into trouble was on the *hurtigruten* ("fast route"), the steamer from Stokmarknes to Trondheim. I found a red button on the wall in the salon in first class, where we weren't supposed to be. We were steerage travelers. I pulled the button, and pushed it, and nothing happened. Then all at once a waiter showed up and in not-so-nice language demanded to know what we wanted. As we stuttered, he chased us out and told us that if he ever saw us again, we would land in the brig. We understood him!

On the train from Trondheim to Oslo, or Kristiania as it was called at that time, Birger and I kept busy. We avoided the conductor at each stop and waited until the last possible minute to climb aboard our car, which was, of course, third class.

There was a locked door between third and first class. At one stop, Birger waited too long and had to jump onto a first-class car. He could not get to us, where Mother was crying and Dad was comforting her. She thought Birger was lost forever.

At the next stop, the conductor brought him to us with a warning to Dad and Mother to tie us down if necessary.

Uncle Kristian met us in Oslo, and we stayed there two or three days before boarding the steamship *Stavangerfjord* for the United States. Sister Ida, as I said before, had to stay behind because of her TB. It was a sad goodbye to her in Oslo, not knowing when or if we would see her again.

Now the Atlantic, for 10 days. Just think: America waiting to receive the Johannessen family!

We were forbidden by Mother and Dad to venture beyond the confines of third class, but I'm afraid this wasn't adhered to. Birger and I explored third class, then second, then first class. The only thing we didn't bother to examine was the anchor chain. Ed was more docile than Birger and I, and Egil was only 6, so Mother watched him more closely, afraid he might fall overboard.

Dad was in his glory, for he was known by several passengers for his song group in Norway and his conducting, and he was asked to

Sister Ida in Kristiania (Oslo), before she joined us in Alaska

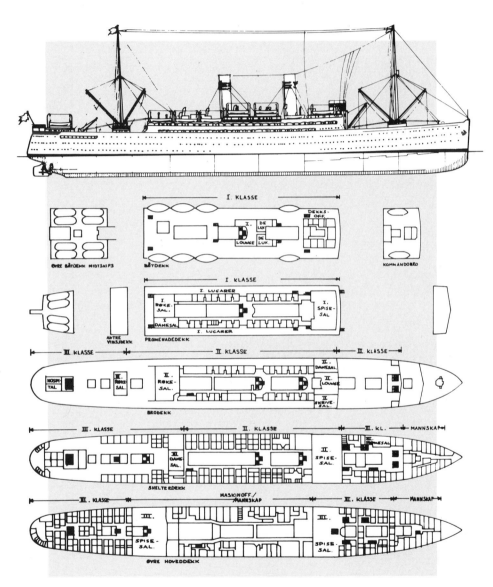

Layout of the *Stavangerfjord* (from *Amerikabåtene, Norsk Sjofartsmuseum*, Oslo, 1984)

organize a singing group on board. My brothers and I were included in some of the songs. Soon we were singing for second- and first-class passengers at mealtimes, and for the officers.

Birger and I were kept so busy we didn't get into much mischief until the last night's performance at the first-class farewell party. I was not required to sing with the group, but I wanted to hear the music, so I sneaked in. The only empty seat was in the front row between two fancily dressed ladies. I proceeded to occupy it as if it had been reserved for me.

I got some haughty looks in my homemade clothes, I'll tell you, from those hotsy-totsy ladies, but it didn't hurt my feelings much. I had already learned that when in doubt about something, the best way was to take the offensive as soon as possible. I just gave the women a couple of dirty looks of my own, and that was the end of that.

I enjoyed listening to the singing, even though Dad scolded me afterward.

We pictured Ellis Island awaiting us, but because of a flu epidemic we landed instead at Manhattan, as I recall. We were allowed to stay aboard the *Stavangerfjord* that night. Next morning, a Lutheran Church organization met the immigrants, and of course the immigration authorities were there and helped get us ashore.

The church group herded us to some kind of down-and-outers' hotel, perhaps a church mission. There we were to wait until one o'clock exactly and then walk to the train. Birger and I disappeared immediately. On the way from the dock to the hotel with the church group, we had seen an aquarium of some kind. We didn't understand the words on the building, but we had seen pictures of fish on it.

Dad had taught us how to line up two or three mountains to have a landmark in order to get to a precise spot on the ocean, so Birger and I took our bearings. We picked three tall buildings, and the sun was out so we knew where north, south, east and west were. No big deal. We wouldn't get lost.

39

But the aquarium was so interesting, we forgot about time. When we came to our senses, we ran like the devil back to the hotel. We knew we were in trouble.

The preacher and all of the immigrants were lined up single file for about a block, the preacher at the head and Mother and Dad last. When we came running down the street, the preacher signaled to get started immediately, so Mother and Dad didn't have time to spank us. We got to the train on time. By then we were forgiven. This time.

The next day we changed trains in Chicago. At a lunch counter near the station, I noticed a jar of something bright yellow on the table. Dad, who liked to kid us, said, "It's good! Have some on your sandwich." So I smeared a lot on my bread and took a big bite. Boy, did I spit it out quickly! That was my introduction to mustard, and to this day I am not fond of it.

For four days on the train—and no sleeping car for us—we were too bushed to get into much mischief. A crowd of soldiers returning from France had a lot of fun teaching us English, including some cuss words. Dad understood English quite well after his time in the Klondike, but he and Mother were too exhausted to realize how we were being entertained.

Arriving in Seattle, we probably looked even more bedraggled than we felt. I remember so well all of us waiting at the railroad station while Dad looked for a hotel for us. He chose one in Pioneer Square that I think was called the Olympic. It's gone now. He wanted to be near the wharf where steamers took off for Alaska, but he soon found out to his disappointment that we could not leave for a couple of months because the mailboat that made the run from Kodiak to Unga Island had disappeared at sea. A new mail contract was to be let by August 25.

Because we didn't have enough money to stay in the hotel for that long a time, he made arrangements for us to go to a farm in

Sumner, about 15 miles south of where the airport is now, and pick berries.

When he and Mother came back to the hotel with Egil to tell us older boys what they had decided, the Japanese manager ordered Dad in no uncertain terms to "get those kids out of here immediately!" This is what had happened:

In the old country, we were used to going swimming every day at that time of year. So the three of us, glad to be off the train, had undressed in our room and filed naked down the hallway to the bathroom, just as if we were at the swimming beach at home. We met several people on the way, some of whom were ladies who screamed and hid their faces. That was their problem. We had our bath and returned dripping wet to our room.

Soon the proprietor knocked on our door. We didn't answer because, lacking towels, we had climbed into bed and covered ourselves with blankets to dry. He came in, exclaiming something in English, I think, although it didn't matter—for us it might as well have been Japanese. We just gawked at him. He grabbed our covers and pulled them off us, then threw up his hands, babbled some more and left the room shaking his head.

He relented and let us stay there that night, and the next morning we went to Sumner on a bus. We were there maybe a month—long enough for me to discover how to train a rooster to get him to charge people. He would fly into their faces. Ed, Birger and I also liked climbing cherry trees, which was another no-no.

So, back to Seattle, where we found another hotel, between Second and Third avenues. We stayed there about two weeks before we were asked to leave because we boys were running too frequently up and down stairs in our homemade shoes with iron wearplates on the heels.

Often, Mother and Dad visited relatives and old friends in Seattle, and we three boys—Egil went with Mother and Dad—were never idle. On the landing of our next hotel was a parrot we loved to tease. I had a long line with a piece of red cloth hooked to one end that I danced in front of the parrot's cage until he screamed like a son-of-a-gun. The darn hook got caught in the cage one day, and I got caught by the manager. That queered that.

Another day Birger and I bummed dimes from somewhere and climbed aboard a streetcar and rode to Woodland Park. We had no money to get back, but we weren't worried. We knew where the hotel was because we could see the Smith Building not far from the hotel. We thought we could follow the streetcar tracks back, but we found out that didn't work when too many Y's on the track came together. We tried to ask directions, but people didn't understand a word of our Norwegian, and they just walked on by. Somehow we found our way back. By this time Mother and Dad were both ready to tear their hair out.

We stayed for a time in one more hotel. Then at last we boarded the steamer Admiral Watson for Alaska.

Finally—the last stretch to what we all thought would be Utopia.

There was a full list of passengers. We, of course, were in steerage. Over the Gulf of Alaska, the steamer hit something and broke a blade off one of the propellers. The rear end of the ship just bounced around, out of balance. We had to go up Cook Inlet to Anchorage. There we tied up for two days at Emard's Dock, where the steamer could go dry at low tide and they could put on a new blade.

From there the ship went on to Kodiak, where we waited a week for the new mailboat, the Bergen.

We set sail from Kodiak in mid-August, nearly three months after leaving Søberg. The Bergen was quite a boat—an old cattle-hauling ship with no staterooms. The sleeping quarters for the passengers, about 20 of us in all, were in the fo'c'sle, with canvas bunks on both sides. The men got together and strung a rope from the bow down to the center of the entrance steps into the fo'c'sle and hung blankets up to divide the area—one side for women and children and the

The Admiral Watson (photo courtesy of Special Collections Division, University of Washington Libraries, negative #14737)

other for the men. Many of the passengers were going all the way to Unalaska, some to Chignik. We were the only ones bound for Unga.

On a wild rainy evening, we left Uyak Bay near the western end of Kodiak for the mainland, to pick up coal for the journey. At the entrance to the coal harbor, west and about 40 miles north of Uyak, I was seasick as the devil. Suddenly we hit a rock, and there was pandemonium for a while. Everyone was piling out of the fo'c'sle at the same time. But Mother refused to budge from her bunk.

She had had enough. "*La båten synke*," she said, for all she cared—"Let the boat sink."

But we slid off the rock without too much damage and landed to take on some coal. Then we departed the same night into the black, stormy weather.

I stayed on deck, sick and heaving over the side until the salt spray soaked me. I didn't return to the fo'c'sle because of the terrible stench down there. I crawled into a lifeboat with a canvas cover, where I stayed all night. Dad said he looked all over the ship for me until someone told him they had seen me crawling into the lifeboat. He just let me stay there.

Five days later, after a stop at Chignik, we entered Unga harbor and dropped anchor. The same day, Uncle Nick arrived in his 40-foot fishing boat, Baby. We all six climbed aboard with him and headed for Hardscratch. Oh boy, oh boy, oh boy! Were we glad to be ending this long voyage, especially Mother and Dad. Even we kids had had our fill of travel.

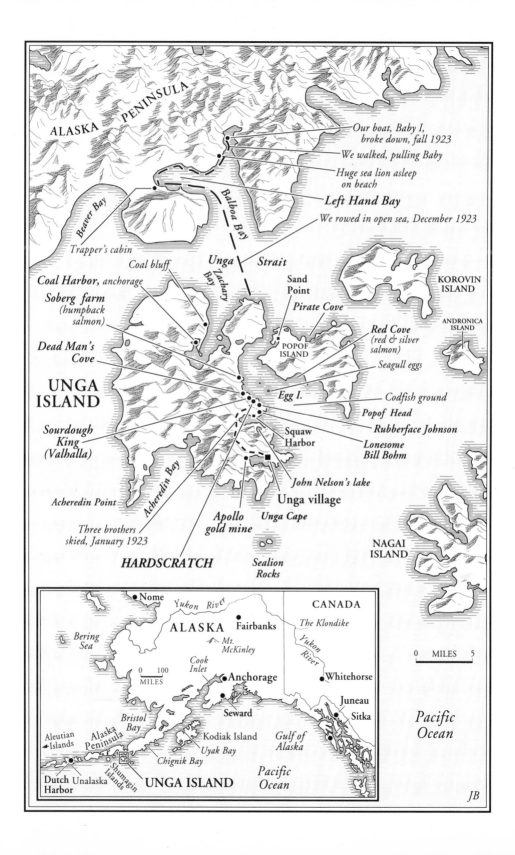

ALASKA PENINSULA

Our boat, Baby I,
broke down, fall 1923

We walked, pulling Baby

Huge sea lion asleep
on beach

Left Hand Bay

We rowed in open sea, December 1923

Beaver Bay

Balboa Bay

Trapper's cabin

Coal bluff

Coal Harbor, anchorage

Soberg farm
(humpback
salmon)

Unga
Zachary
Bay

Unga   Strait

Sand
Point

Pirate Cove

**KOROVIN
ISLAND**

ANDRONICA
ISLAND

Red Cove
(red & silver
salmon)

**Dead Man's
Cove**

POPOF
ISLAND

Seagull eggs

**UNGA
ISLAND**

Egg I.

— **Codfish ground**

Popof Head

**Sourdough
King**
(Valhalla)

Squaw
Harbor

Rubberface Johnson

**Lonesome
Bill Bohm**

Acheredin Bay

John Nelson's lake

Unga village

Acheredin Point

*Three brothers
skied, January 1923*

*Apollo
gold mine*

Unga Cape

**NAGAI
ISLAND**

HARDSCRATCH

*Sealion
Rocks*

0   MILES   5

• Nome   *Yukon River*   CANADA

*Bering
Sea*

ALASKA   • Fairbanks   *The Klondike*

*Mt.
McKinley*

*Yukon
River*

*Cook
Inlet*

• **Anchorage**   • Whitehorse

0   100
MILES

• Seward   • Juneau
• Sitka

*Bristol
Bay*

Kodiak Island   *Gulf of
Alaska*

*Pacific
Ocean*

Aleutian
Islands

Alaska
Peninsula

Uyak Bay

Chignik Bay

UNGA ISLAND

*Pacific
Ocean*

Dutch
Harbor   Unalaska   Shumagin
Islands

JB

4.

Unga Island

Uncle's house had three bedrooms and a bathtub with a hot water tank. The coil went into the kitchen stove, and a water line came from a dam 500 feet west of the fishermen's bunkhouse. Uncle hired half a dozen men for the cod season, late February to May.

The Edna Watts was lying on the beach in front of the bunkhouse, where she had blown ashore during a winter storm, with three holes in her belly and broken ribs.

The bunkhouse had an outhouse nearby, and there was a three-hole outhouse 75 feet west of the main house. On the beach was a shed for wood and coal, as well as a dock for unloading fish, fish-drying racks and a salt house, carpenter shed and net house.

(Early in the gray cod season, the cod would be hung on the racks until dry, about six weeks. Toward the end of the season, because of the arrival of too many flies, the cod catch was salted.

Brailing salmon

47

During red salmon season, we fished at Red Cove on Popof Island. That catch was salted in 200-gallon tanks and later repacked in barrels to be shipped with the *stokkfisk*, the dried cod, which by then had been pressed into 3-foot-square bundles of about 100 pounds each.

(By September or October, a Bristol Bay codfish schooner would anchor at Hardscratch and take the yearly catches to Seattle. That was for us the end of the fishing season.)

Our family arrived in time to help with preparations for winter 1919. We cut a lot of alders, gathered driftwood and dug coal at Coal Harbor, on the north end of Unga Island. After that first year or so, when we had gotten settled on "the farm," as the islanders called our dairy, we also cut wild hay for the cows we acquired and packed it into the hay shed. The only other farm on the island was the Hansons', near Squaw Harbor, and both were strictly dairy farms. Our only crops were vegetables for the family.

Just as in Norway, of course, all year there were chickens and calves to be fed, cows to be milked and cheese and butter to be made. We had a hand-operated churn for making butter. We were never out of work to do, believe me.

Preserving food was always a problem. A lot had to be salted or dried, same as in the old country. In the early winter, we cut ice blocks from a pond above Hardscratch, a spot 50 or 60 feet across in a swamp, and buried them in sawdust in an old ice house at Uncle's place. Chicken eggs, milk, ptarmigan and ducks were plentiful. They were stored in separate containers in the ice house. We used seagull eggs, too. They were put in a barrel with plenty of rock salt.

Toilet paper I never saw in Hardscratch, nor even purchased in Norway. There, we and the neighbors all had small barns with an outhouse in the hayshed corner, alongside the cows. This was pretty sensible. The odor was mixed with others, which was a blessing. At Hardscratch, we always had Sears and Montgomery Ward catalogs for paper, and lime to sprinkle in the outhouse.

To get coal, we had to take Baby to Coal Harbor, about 20 miles

Uncle Nick, Ida, Mother and Dad at Hardscratch

away, where we anchored the boat behind a sand spit and walked the five miles to the coal vein. On the way to the harbor, we would row in to the coal site with a skiff and drop off supplies and a tent in which to live while we dug the coal and packed it in salt sacks.

The coal veins were in a high white bluff that kept sloughing off sand and mud as well as coal. There were several veins 15 or 20 feet apart. The face of the bluff was very steep, so the coal had to be dug out, rolled down the bluff and sacked up later. It was a messy job.

Near the anchorage at Coal Harbor were some old houses and an old shaft coal mine, where coal had been mined in the 1890s for sailing ships from Seattle and San Francisco that hauled prospectors and supplies to Nome during the gold strike.

My brother Eivind (Ed)

It was a poor grade of coal. We had as many ashes as the coal that burned in the stove, but they helped keep the fire going longer.

Andrew Grosvold, the store owner at Sand Point, sold us our first cow, already with a calf due in six months.

To get the cow to Hardscratch was not easy. We could not put her in the hold of Baby, as Uncle didn't have a strong boom on Baby, nor did he have a boom on the dock to hoist a cow out of the hold.

50

So we put the cow on the deck and tied her down. At Hardscratch, about five miles from Sand Point, we shoved her overboard and she swam ashore. There's always more than just one way, isn't there?

That was our beginning with cattle. Later we bought four or five more from an elderly Danish couple four miles north of Hardscratch. Eventually we bought them out and operated our dairy on that strip of land, which extended a mile or so along the beach and half a mile inland. Dad and I mostly took care of this, while Mother cooked for Uncle's fishermen crew. I helped Mother or Dad or whoever was there at the time with the milking and butchering. Ed and Birger, now called Fred, fished for Uncle in separate power dories. People owned power dories out there like people most places now own cars. It was individual transportation by our highway, the sea.

One sunny September day, I led a 2-year-old barren cow to a tripod we had erected, where we could hoist an animal into the air with a tackle after it was killed so we could do the butchering. Usually Dad was there, but this time only Mother was at the farm. I was alone when I started this job. I shot the cow in the head but not where I should have. She broke loose and ran down to the beach and into the salt water up to her belly. I couldn't kill her there because I wouldn't be able to get her up to the tripod and butcher her properly—quarter the meat and handle it in and out of the dory.

I yelled for Mother, and she came right away. My good old mother—she always did. We had a heck of a time trying to drag the cow up to the tripod to finish a poorly executed job. It almost made me and Mother sick. Like many of our animals, the poor cow had been a kind of pet. We finally managed to complete the chore.

Let me tell you, Mother was some lady. She was kind, patient and always calm and helpful. How she could have done the things she did! I can just see her laying me in the feed bin when I came along. She simply did whatever had to be done. Mother, I salute you!

Once when I was chopping wood, I cut the thumb on my left hand nearly off. The bone was split and broken and just dangling.

Mother with Thomas Lauritzen, brother of my future wife, Ruth

Mother straightened it the best she could and wrapped it against my forefinger. There were no doctors within a thousand miles. I lost the use of the muscle in my thumb joint. It has hampered me all my life. No more playing the guitar!

The island was a desolate place: no trees except alders, crooked as a snake, lots of swampy ground, a few mountains—the tallest only 2,000 feet, lots of wind and rain. And Hardscratch was horribly lonesome for us kids at our age. It's a wonder we didn't get into more trouble than we did.

One day, Mother walked the four miles from the farm to Hardscratch and at Dead Man's Cove sat down on a dry knoll to eat a sandwich. She felt something under her hand and dug into the moss. She removed a piece of rotten board and, oh Lord, under it was a skeleton.

When Fred and I heard this, we beat it up there and removed the skull. We put it in a bag and brought it to Hardscratch. But we were instructed, in rather strong words, to return it, re-cover the coffin with some new lumber, and place a cross on the top.

Another of our misadventures only Fred and I ever knew about. Fred had a cast-iron blank .22 pistol. We ran out of blank cartridges and acquired, who knows where, .22 cartridges with real bullets. We discovered that the barrel on the revolver was bored from both ends and that the hole did not meet exactly in the center, so we bored it out in Uncle's shop. This worked fine. We shot at everything in sight, without hurting anyone or anything. But eventually our ammunition ran out.

We somehow got some .22 specials, which are longer and larger than regulars. We had to rebore the barrel again. We couldn't reach through the barrel, so we cut it off in the middle. Now we got cautious. We clamped the revolver in a vise in the carpenter shop, tied a string to the trigger and stood clear. The first shot exploded in fragments of cast iron everywhere. We considered it a good lesson in being careful.

The winter of 1922-23 we had a lot of snow, and we three boys skied the 12 miles to Unga village. That's when I first met my future wife, Ruth Lauritzen, whose parents also had come from Norway. She was 9 years old at the time.

That year or the year after, she came to Hardscratch for a visit and stayed with us for a couple of days, until her father and mother picked her up in their dory. She has always said that she enjoyed the visit but that while my two older brothers were pleasant and kind, I was rough and an awful tease. Over the years, she and I ran into each other two or three times, here and there in Alaska. Twenty-five years after that first meeting, we met again, fell in love and got married. She said she married me to get even. Well, we just passed our 44th wedding anniversary. How long does it take to get even?

The winter we skied to Unga, we were there for Russian Christmas. Beginning on the seventh of January, there was a big celebration for seven days—masquerades and a dance, and a lot of people got pretty high on sourdough home brew or whatever they could find to drink.

The elderly schoolteacher at Unga was Miss Clark. She never married. I don't remember the young teacher's name. For the masquerade, Miss Clark and the younger teacher dressed me up as a high school graduate with a mortarboard on my head, the only one I ever had in my life. It was one I certainly never earned. I was 14, but I was tall, nearly six feet. Ed and Fred and I still could barely speak English. The Unga children snickered at us at first, but we had a marvelous time.

Miss Clark had a real nice cat, a female with red and white stripes. I remember it well. The next summer, Miss Clark's cat showed up at our farm, of all places. Miss Clark had left for Chignik, where she was going to be teaching that fall.

I had the wanderlust that year. I had a chance to go to Kodiak with a man named Opheim, who had a boat built by Uncle exactly like our Baby and had it shipped on the new mailboat, the Starr (later skippered by Captain Chris Trondsen, who now occasionally

54

Unga village (photo courtesy of the Ben Stewart family)

lets me beat him at pool in his basement in Ballard). I boxed up Miss Clark's cat and delivered it to her at Chignik on the way to Kodiak. Was she happy!

For the rest of that summer, 1923, I dug razor clams at Kukak Beach, near the Valley of Ten Thousand Smokes in what is now the Katmai National Park, on the mainland across from Kodiak Island. I bummed my way back home in early September.

At Hardscratch we had a cat of our own, who disappeared one summer. After three weeks, we decided she was gone forever. At the time, we were patching up a hole on the inside planking—the double

55

Uncle Nick and Ruth at Hardscratch

skin, it's called—of the Edna Watts. One day while I was sweeping inside the hull where we had been working, I heard a faint sound and finally located where it seemed to be coming from. I went and got Uncle right away. We cut a hole, and sure enough—the cat came crawling out, skinny as a dried codfish. It survived OK. Now there's a cat with nine lives!

When you live on the ocean, you always know where the tide is or should be. One day in 1923, shortly after I got back from Kodiak, the tide was about half out when I went down to the barn to gather eggs. When I got back from the barn after taking care of the chickens, the tide was already coming back in again. I watched it for a while, wondering what was happening. When it got over the sand spit, I rushed back to the barn and shooed the chickens up into the hay loft. The cows were out foraging. I had no idea what was going on.

When the water went over the spit and about four feet deep into the barn, I thought of the neighbors south of us whose house was on the same level as the barn. I jumped into the skiff and rowed to their house, tied the skiff to the handle of their door and reached over and opened the door. A washtub came floating out with a small dog and a cat in it. Now the tide seemed to sit still. I waited, and finally it started back out.

Almost three months later, we found out about the Japanese earthquake and tidal wave that had done great damage many places. In our area, wharves had floated off, but as it was an otherwise calm day, nothing too serious happened.

That fall, a fisherman friend of Uncle's needed someone to transport him to Portage Bay on the mainland so he could walk over the mail carrier's trail to Herendeen Bay on the Bering Sea side of the peninsula.

Tom Devine, a fisherman at Hardscratch, volunteered to transport Uncle's friend with Baby and to take along a man named John Vosstrand, who had come from Duluth the year before to fish for Uncle. Vosstrand wanted to go to Left Hand Bay to try his hand at trapping, and I asked to go along.

After we landed Uncle's friend at Portage Bay, the engine on Baby broke down. We had to walk the beach and pull the boat by a long rope the whole 15 miles to Left Hand Bay, where Vosstrand had rented a trapline and cabin. Tom Devine was on board steering, to keep Baby from going on the beach, and Vosstrand and I were on the beach pulling hard and not looking very far ahead. Tom yelled at us to watch out—and there we were, almost stepping on a sea lion that was asleep on the sand. The lion let out a bawl you could hear for miles that scared the gee whiz out of us for sure. The rest of the haul was uneventful. It took two days.

I enjoyed trapping with John Vosstrand until near Christmas. This was just an exploratory trip for him, so we didn't intend to stay too long. We went back to Hardscratch in a rowing dory that Tom Devine had towed to Left Hand Bay for us. We had a makeshift sail,

Codfish drying at Coal Harbor

but we rowed most of the way, because these flat-bottom boats aren't built to be sailed too well except before the wind.

This was a dangerous time of the year, cold, when Bristol Bay storms are very strong and unpredictable. We made it just fine, though.

On the trapline one day, Vosstrand shot a red fox through the eye at a great distance. He was a good shot for a cheechako—he shot eagles on the wing with his rifle. At that time, it was OK with the government to shoot eagles. In fact, he got a bounty of $10 a pair for the claws, because the eagles were killing a lot of the salmon.

We had some peculiar neighbors on Unga Island, with some peculiar names. Anybody up there who had a quirk of any kind got nicknamed immediately.

A Union Fish Co. crew at Unga: Conrad Lauritzen (left),
Charlie Ottesen, "Svoger" Oberg and Scotty Reeves

I remember well Wild Bill the Patagonian, who had been shang-haied as a little boy from the Strait of Magellan on a square-rigger. He served as a cabin boy on ships and later worked as a cook. Somehow he wound up in the Shumigans.

One season I had someone helping me bundle dried cod with the *stokkfisk* press on the north end of the island, and Wild Bill cooked for us. He taught me some table manners. At supper one night, I scraped butter off my knife back onto the butter dish. Wild Bill sternly inquired who had done this. I got the idea—my cheeks still burn!

When Wild Bill looked at you, you got scared. One of his eyes went straight up into his head. It was eerie to look at him.

The Fiddler was a man named John Martin, who played at the dances and various celebrations at Sand Point and Unga. I loved to dance.

"Vasekopp" was a Norwegian whose nickname means he talked fast—half in English, half in Norwegian, with a lisp. You could hardly understand him.

There was Dago Mike, the Italian, and John Iverson, who never closed his fly. When asked, he said, "It's Handy Laddy."

And there was Fred the Whaler and Pete the Sneller, and Frenchie, a dark French North African. And Lofoten—a Norwegian, of course. When he talked, he spit tobacco juice that dribbled down from both sides of his mouth. Danish Pete Larsen, Mexican Frank Rodgers. They loved telling their stories, and we loved hearing them. Wild Bill supposedly was from a man-eating tribe in Patagonia, and he looked like it.

This was my schooling. It sure gave me itchy feet.

Near Hardscratch was a place they called Valhalla, or Viking Heaven, owned by a man nicknamed the Sourdough King because he always had several 33-gallon barrels of the stuff brewing. I say 33 gallons because that was the size of the salmon barrels everybody used for home brew.

Sourdough was made by mixing flour, water, yeast and lots of sugar. When it got brewing well, they mixed in dried fruits or anything else that might help it, until it quit bubbling (got "brewed out"). By then, the sediment had settled to the bottom, and the fruit floated on the milky liquor at the top. It tasted like something halfway between wine and I don't know what else. What the alcohol level was, I also don't know, but it must have been fairly strong. (Of course, some people used their sourdough starter strictly for baking.)

Some of the old-timers would gather and get gloriously drunk

The mailboat Starr at Unga

on the brew for weeks at a time. When a particular supply was gone, they would move to another place and repeat. This went on all winter.

You must remember, we had not much diversion up there. We certainly didn't have TV, and we didn't have radio. The only outside contact we had was the newspapers, which we got fairly regularly once a month except for the two or three months in the winter when the mailboat was in Seattle getting overhauled.

So all there was to pass the winter with was chopping wood and shooting ptarmigan and ducks for food. Everybody just ran out of things to do.

It was my job in the morning to bring the cows in to be milked.

Fred Pomian ("Fred the Whaler"), at Unga in 1962 (photo courtesy of his granddaughter, Martha Hunt Fletcher)

I was not permitted to go alone anywhere near Valhalla when the bunch were enjoying their sourdough mix. One morning the cows were up in the Sourdough King's area, so Fred went with me. We found two cows that had gotten into the sourdough barrels, which the Sourdough King kept in a shed with hay stacked around them to keep them warm. The cows were lying on the ground outside the shed, straight-legged and bloated like a couple of bass drums. We pounded on their bellies, but although their eyes were wide open, they were out.

We ran over to the house. Inside and out, it was a mess. We peeked through the bedroom window and saw a man we knew named Oscar Sande apparently sleeping, but with his eyes open. Just then, a woman called One-Eyed Lena came in. She had bruises all over her face and her arms. Her good eye was blackened—she was blind in the other. They evidently had had quite a fight.

One-Eyed Lena had a cat in her hands. So help me, she placed the cat on Oscar's face and pulled it by the tail down to his chest. He jumped up with a scream.

Fred and I ran like the devil for home, where Dad grabbed a butcher knife and came with us to take care of the cows. The animals were too far gone, bloated with colic, so we just butchered them right there. But the meat was no good. We could taste the sourdough in it. We disposed of it by heaving it in the ocean.

Another neighbor half a mile south was called Rubberface Johnson. He had such a big mouth he could swallow his nose. Rubberface heard that we would like to have a small calf castrated. Dad had never done this, either in the old country or at Hardscratch.

"Rubberface" Johnson (photo courtesy of Alice Nilson)

"The Fiddler," John Martin, with Lena Jorgensen,
Ruth's grandmother, and Ruth's brother Billy

Rubberface said, "Heck, there's nothing to it. I'll do it for you right now—it will just take a minute. Bring a basin full of water and some Lysol."

Before I knew it, while Dad held the calf down, Rubberface bent down and bit the whole thing off. The poor calf took off, bawling like something you wouldn't believe. Its mother was waiting for it.

"This is how it was done for years by the Basque people in Spain," said Rubberface. (We called him another name after that.)

Finally, there was Lonesome Kraut, a German by the name of Bill Bohm, who lived half a mile south of Rubberface, about a mile from Hardscratch. He was so excessively clean he followed visitors to the door with a mop. We could never go in with our shoes on. He always wore a white shirt, and he was a compulsive cleaner, continually cleaning his house. Nothing was ever clean enough for him.

He got tired of moving things to clean, so he built another house alongside his old one and lived in it in the winter, then moved back to his old house in the summer. The houses were just for himself. He had no one. He certainly could have had a woman, but he was just by himself. He was an old cook who had worked in various canneries and other places.

Lonesome failed to show up at a place he was supposed to visit one day, and the man went to look for him. Lonesome had put a lot of old newspapers all over the floor so he wouldn't make any mess. He was sitting on a chair, leaning on a small table with a revolver lying on the table where it had fallen after he shot himself in the mouth. There was blood all over the walls and ceiling, but he had saved the floor with the newspapers.

Lonesome left a will, and in it he left his gun to a man named Bill Johnson, a cannery watchman near Sand Spit at Sand Point. Two years later, Bill Johnson did the same thing Lonesome had done, with the same gun.

On another morning when I was fetching the cows for milking, I happened to look toward Red Cove and Egg Island, where we gathered seagull eggs, and saw smoke rolling up from a fire on the island. I woke up Uncle Nick, who guessed correctly that it must be a signal for help.

We went over with Baby, in a 30- to 40-mile southeast wind that was blowing rain before it, and found five men, cold and wet. They were black from smoke, their eyes red.

It turned out to be my future wife's father, Hjalmar Lauritzen, and some fishermen. They had been returning from Pirate Cove when the engine room on their gasoline-powered tender caught fire. This was the Lasco #1 from San Francisco, owned by the Union Fish Co., which Hjalmar was in charge of at Unga. They had abandoned ship because of the danger of explosion, and their dory had

Hjalmar Lauritzen, Ruth's father, with his cat Tony and John Berntsen Sr., known as John the Sneller ("Snailer"), at Unga (photo courtesy of Alice Nilson)

broken up on the beach when they tried to land in the breakers.

We took them back to Hardscratch, where Mother fed them, and they walked to Unga the same day. The Lasco #1 landed on a beach OK and didn't burn.

Uncle Nick eventually built a Baby #2, larger than Baby #1. He sent to Sweden for a one-cylinder Bollinder diesel engine, but then he couldn't get any diesel fuel. He built a wood tank where we put all our cod livers to rot, and the resulting oil was used in place of diesel fuel. What a stink! And it smoked like a volcano.

Conrad Lauritzen, one of Hjalmar Lauritzen's sons, used the Baby #2 one year, shortly before Uncle Nick passed away. Finally it was left on the beach at Unga Bay lagoon, near where the Edna Watts had burned up some years before. I don't know what happened to Baby #1.

The gray cod season the winter of 1924-25 was not good. Dad and I fished for Uncle Nick along with Ed and Fred, all in separate dories. Mother cooked. Toward spring, Dad and I fished by ourselves for codfish, which we salted, taking off from our own little dock at the farm so we could keep an eye on things at home.

When we got news that fish sent the year before had sold for less than the cost of the freight to Seattle, I said, "Enough." Fred and I bought tickets to Kodiak on the Starr for the 10th of May. He was 19, I was 17.

Dad took this very hard.

The day Fred and I left Hardscratch, we ran the power dory from the farm to Hardscratch to say goodbye to Mother and Uncle and pick up Ed to take us to Sand Point. Mother cried and hugged us so hard. She suspected we would never return.

Heading back to the farm on the way to Sand Point, we met Dad, who was on his way to Hardscratch to tell us goodbye. The weather was calm, and we tied the two dories up side by side. Fred

and I climbed into Dad's dory. There were hard hugs.

With tears in his eyes, Dad said, "I will never see you boys again." That surprised me. "Be careful," he said.

I'll never forget. He had tried so hard to find Utopia. Instead, he found Hardscratch. He passed away alone on the farm two weeks after Fred and I left, and word didn't get to us until weeks after that. He is buried on a hill overlooking the farm and Hardscratch.

Survival
on
Montague
Island

My brother Fred took this shot of me in the crowded tent on Montague

Survival on
Montague Island

We are born with a survival instinct, but adverse conditions hone and sharpen it.

In the old country, 200 miles north of the Arctic Circle where I was born and grew up through grade school, life could be harsh. Especially in winter, survival was a constant lesson.

And at Hardscratch, our family's settlement on Unga Island, we had more survival practice, fishing for cod in open boats in midwinter. We learned to be good sailors and weather observers under unpredictable conditions and with primitive equipment. In fog or snow, waves and wind substituted for a compass.

After my brother Fred and I left Hardscratch as teenagers in early 1925, we spent the summer working on separate cannery tenders and herring purse-seine boats around Cook Inlet, Kodiak Island and Prince William Sound. We were both mechanically inclined enough to wind up as engineers, which on those rigs were really glorified oilers.

Although our formal education had been cut short when we left Norway, we had done quite a bit of mechanical work in the Shumagins around engines in various small boats and, of course, had had considerable experience fishing. We were pretty good boatmen.

The fishing season was over in Prince William Sound about the middle of September. I had written Fred that I would be looking for work in the Latouche mine and that I would stick around and wait for him to get to Latouche, hoping he would arrive within a week or so.

While hanging around the poolroom at a boarding house, I struck up an acquaintance with a man, Sam Elstead, who had just come from Manley Hot Springs on the Yukon River. He was about 35 years old and had been prospecting and trapping for several years. We soon developed a friendship that continued for many years.

When Fred appeared on the scene at Latouche, Sam and I had already discussed the possibility of trapping mink or marten or whatever was in the area for the winter. We were especially interested in the Port Wells country, or in looking for land otter on Montague Island. After considerable discussion, and with little prospect of jobs in the mine, the three of us agreed that Montague offered the best possibilities for making a few dollars.

Sam and Fred had somewhere between two and three hundred dollars each, I about five hundred. I had been luckier than Fred fishing. We pooled our resources and made a list of everything we would need—groceries, traps, a skiff, etc. Few supplies for a trapping expedition such as ours would be available in a strictly company-owned mining town, so it was agreed that Sam and I would go to Seward on an Alaska Steamship steamer. That would take about three days—one day up, a day to purchase an outfit, and a day to get back to Latouche.

While we were gone, Fred was to make arrangements for a small fishing boat to take us to Montague Island. In addition, he was to secure the small skiff we would need for our own use. We would be depending on ducks and possibly a seal or two for our fresh meat and would also need a boat for exploring the coast and for fishing, to supplement our diet. We knew there were no deer on the island and the brown bear would be hibernating soon. This was almost the first of October and snow was due any time. (Incidentally, two years

Sam Elstead and Fred Soberg a few years after Montague

later deer were successfully planted on the island.)

We expected to be a good team, for Sam was experienced in the woods as a trapper, and Fred and I were the sailors and fishermen.

While in Seward, Sam and I took in some night life, and a movie that we never forgot—"Sinners in Heaven," about an airplane flying from England to Australia that runs out of gas and makes a forced landing on a palm-tree island. Only the pilot and a gorgeous young woman survive. Although we didn't remember the actors' names,

Sam and I had many happy moments talking about that movie.

Our outfit cost around a thousand dollars. After purchasing an eight-foot skiff and chartering a fishing boat to take us to Port Chalmers on Montague Island, we were broke.

We made specific arrangements with the fisherman. He was to come back and check on us about the first of December. By then we would know whether it would pay to stick it out for what would probably be better trapping in January or February.

On the first of October 1925, we left Latouche for Port Chalmers, a 35-mile trip that took about five hours.

This part of Prince William Sound is known to be very choppy in the fall and winter, for the wind has a straight sweep from Columbia Glacier and Valdez Arm from the north and the Gulf of Alaska from the south. About the only protection is Green Island, a small fox-farming island at the time, 10 miles or so west of Port Chalmers. We couldn't know then just what sort of protection it would eventually offer.

The weather looked unsettled and stormy, but we had a good crossing. With only a poor map of the 40-mile-long island and no charts to tell us anything about the coastline, we made a wild guess at where to land and dropped hook near a small river in the Port Chalmers area, toward the northern end of Montague, on the west side.

We now discovered that Port Chalmers was a very poor harbor for a small boat, especially at that time of year. Because the skipper of the boat was anxious about getting back to Latouche, we hurriedly unloaded supplies onto the skiff and made a trip ashore. Fred and I had begun to see that Sam was not a very good boatman, so Fred took him ashore with part of the supplies and then Fred and I rowed the rest in.

Sam picked a likely spot for a temporary camp, not far from a creek near some spruce trees. By the time we got the tent pitched, with spruce boughs for padding under our blankets, it was getting dark and the fishing boat had disappeared toward Latouche. By 7 o'clock we were fairly snug, cooking supper on our Yukon camp stove and enjoying it. Our gear was stored about five feet or more above the level of the creek and probably 50 or 60 feet back from the bank, but maybe a couple of feet lower than the tent. A southeast wind was beginning to blow and the night was very dark, with ugly clouds traveling fast. Now Fred and I learned that Sam could see little or nothing as soon as darkness fell. He always kept a flashlight handy for this reason.

To sleep warmer—there were no sleeping bags in 1925—and to take less room in the small tent, we spread our blankets together on one bed. At 10 or 11 o'clock, it started raining hard, but we were fast asleep by midnight after our strenuous day.

Around 3 in the morning we were awakened by water running through our bedding. Luckily we had not undressed before turning in, so we were on deck in one hell of a hurry. The first discovery was that all of the supplies stacked outside the tent under a tarp had disappeared, including the skiff. With only Sam's flashlight to work by, we hastily tore down the tent and moved it and our remaining gear to higher ground, along with the groceries that had been in the tent. This turned out to be quite a chore, for the wind was blowing a gale, the rain was streaming down, and the night was as black as Billy-be-damned. All we could do under the circumstances was pile everything in a heap, put the tent over it, and crawl under the tent ourselves and wait for daylight.

We were soaked to the skin. Our blankets—in fact, all our things—were soaking wet. It rained for three days, but the level of the creek went down as the rain slowed. Judging by what we could see or find, this was more water than the creek had held for many, many years. We surmised there had been a cloudburst in the mountains, the watershed for the area.

The first day, we found the skiff, which hadn't drifted very far, plus the tarp, Fred's $100 violin, and other things that floated. The trip hadn't done the violin much good.

We re-established our camp and proceeded to dry things out, a very slow process with only the Yukon stove. As the water receded, we kept salvaging what we could of our possessions. The traps and other sinkable stuff couldn't have gone very far but were probably buried in the gravel. Canned goods were scattered several hundred feet down-river. They had rolled on the bottom and the labels were gone. This was a nuisance later—we never knew what was in a can until we opened it.

Most of the staples were dried beans, split peas, rice and some

Fred played violin with a group of friends in Juneau

78

fruit—dried prunes, raisins, apples—in paper bags, and about 50 pounds of sugar and 100 pounds of flour in cotton and burlap bags. The flour floated to shore with the violin. Water had soaked in so far that, after drying it, we had about four inches of usable core left in the center of each of the 50-pound bags. The sugar was soaked through and eventually dried up into a chunk about the size of a football. Most of the dried fruit had floated away and disappeared. Rice and split peas were mixed with sand and gravel, salvageable if we could find them. Those we could find we cleaned off and saved to be rationed out later.

Shotgun shells, paper, cartridges, rifle and .22 shells were all OK—except that the shotgun shells had swelled up so they would not go in the gun. Every one of them had to be scraped with a knife to fit the gun.

After everything we could salvage was picked up, we took inventory. Even by carefully rationing so much a day, we had very few provisions left for two months—and that was assuming we got lots of ducks.

Shortly after we had set up this first camp, Sam explored the country 10 miles north and south for a permanent location. It was determined that the best area for land otter was six miles north of the first camp, on some saltwater lagoons with a 10-mile valley or natural pass leading to a long, narrow bay—Zaikof Bay—on the north end of Montague.

It was now about the 10th of October, and we were ready to move when the tide was right. Next morning looked like a fair day ahead so we tore down the camp and started loading up. To get into the lagoon where Sam thought we should build our log cabin, we would need a high tide, which would be around 4 o'clock that afternoon. We knew we probably would not make more than two miles an hour, for the skiff would be riding not more than four inches above the waterline, loaded with all our stuff and two men. Sam would walk.

At daylight, about 8 a.m., the tide was close to being at its lowest. It took quite a while to get everything packed and stored just right and covered with a tarp. Around 11 we were ready. As we had foreseen, we had only about four inches of freeboard and would have to be extra careful.

Sam looked worried. He said he would try to follow the beach as much as possible to keep track of us, but the rocky shoreline, full of boulders, would slow him down. We thought he should take the straightest course to be sure to get there before dark. We parted and set out, Fred and I rowing, Sam walking.

We had to bail a lot. There were cross swells in the open water and the wind was blowing a little on shore. The waves kept slopping over the side and progress was slow.

Not once after we started did we see Sam. By late afternoon we came to the outer lagoon. To our consternation, the tide was running like the mill-tails of hell through a narrow neck into the lagoon. We turned around and looked the situation over, rowing against the incoming current, and clung to the entrance for a while until the tide seemed to calm down a bit. Then we went through the gap backward, one of us bailing hard to keep from sinking. The water channeling into the next two lagoons was also swift but was more easily managed because it was sheltered and had no wave action. In the upper lagoon, where Sam had previously blazed some trees, we found a natural landing spot for unloading.

It was after 4 o'clock or so and no sign of Sam. We unloaded the skiff and proceeded to erect the tent. When darkness arrived, we began to worry. The weather had cleared. By the time we had the camp ready, somewhere near 7 o'clock, the moon came out, making a beautiful evening. Every once in a while we would walk outside and yell as loudly as we could and fire a shot from the 300 Savage, but we got no answer.

By midnight it started to freeze. We got more and more worried that something serious had happened to Sam—maybe a tangle with a brown bear. He had only the .22 rifle with him, hoping to get some ptarmigan along the way.

We slept very little that night. Come daybreak we were ready to look for Sam. We fixed extra food, put some dry clothing in a packsack, got the rifle and shotgun ready, and then, just as we were setting out, we heard a yell. It was Sam.

He came through the woods up to the tent, a sorry-looking creature. His clothes were wet and semi-frozen. We helped him undress and put on dry clothes, and we fed him. He told us he had tried to follow the shoreline to keep an eye on us but lost track of us when we rounded some point or other. Then he got worried we might have swamped. After a while he turned back to see if anything had drifted ashore from our load on the skiff, for there was that light on-shore breeze. All of this had made him late and he hurried north again, toward our new campsite. When it started getting dark, he was in trouble: He didn't have his flashlight. Stumbling through the timber, brush and swamp, he fell into a huge pothole and lost his .22.

He realized then he would never find camp. It was impossible to build a fire because everything was still wet from all the rain we had had. So, when the moon came up, he started walking back and forth between two trees to keep warm. When he heard the shots we had fired, he was so happy he didn't mind his predicament at all. He didn't hear our shouts, so he decided to stay where he was until morning. The freezing didn't bother him too much. As soon as daylight permitted, he set out and found us.

That day was spent getting camp comfortable and cutting wood. The next day, while Fred remained in camp, Sam and I backtracked Sam's trail to try to find the .22. It was a slow process, for Sam had gotten quite confused from the ordeal. After a couple of hours, I

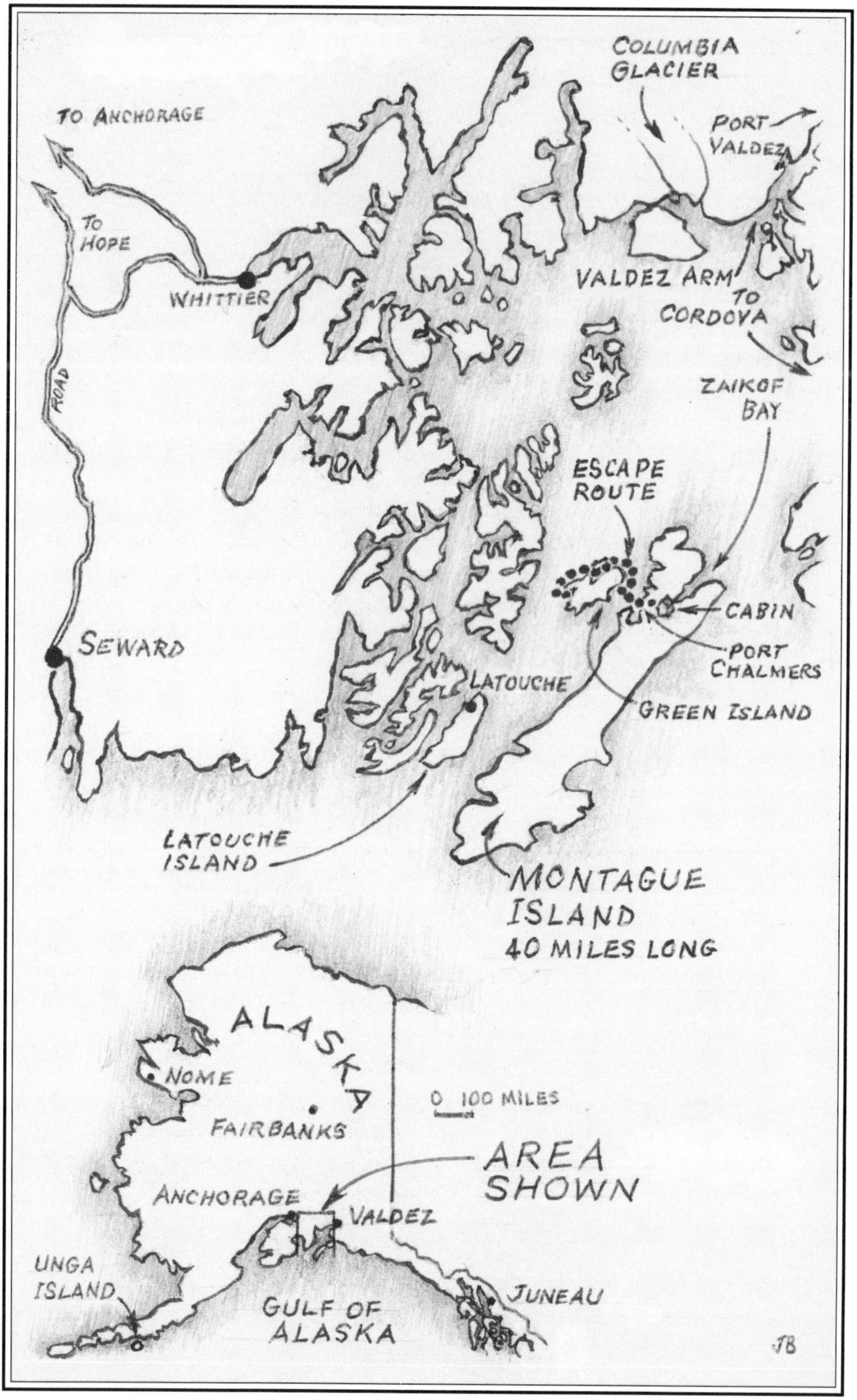

TO ANCHORAGE

TO HOPE

ROAD

WHITTIER

COLUMBIA GLACIER

PORT VALDEZ

VALDEZ ARM

TO CORDOVA

ZAIKOF BAY

ESCAPE ROUTE

CABIN

PORT CHALMERS

GREEN ISLAND

SEWARD

LATOUCHE

LATOUCHE ISLAND

MONTAGUE ISLAND
40 MILES LONG

ALASKA

NOME

FAIRBANKS

0 100 MILES

AREA SHOWN

ANCHORAGE

VALDEZ

UNGA ISLAND

GULF OF ALASKA

JUNEAU

JB

stumbled onto a short, well-worn trail, maybe 40 feet long, between a couple of trees. Not realizing what it signified, I yelled to Sam, "Holy Christ, there's deer on this island! Come take a look."

Of course, as soon as Sam saw it, he said, "Yes, I'm the deer. And there's the hole I fell into." After half an hour of fishing in the hole—a good five feet deep and eight feet long—with a piece of wire, we retrieved the rifle and headed home.

Sam, a college graduate from Denmark with a very dry sense of humor, was seemingly devoid of ego. A tough outdoorsman, he never panicked. He had nicknames for everyone. Fred was "the Professor" because he always argued with Sam about the English language and he looked like a professor. In fact, when he had a goatee I thought Fred looked like Trotsky. I became "the Physician," for I had the knack of improvising in many emergencies and I resembled a physician, Sam said. For some reason, no one ever nicknamed Sam. He was a fine man.

I avoided heavy labor whenever possible. Lazy, I guess. So, I was elected to do most of the duck hunting. I developed into a first-class hunter. Sometimes I would wait patiently for hours for the ducks to line up and get five or six in one shot. Fred hunted some, too. He was good at carpentry, so he and Sam did most of the hewing and fitting of the logs for the cabin now under construction.

On nice days, Sam explored in preparation for trapping season. Fishing turned out to be a fizzle. Fred and I tried our luck several times but were skunked. When the tides were right for getting out of the lagoon, the weather was too nasty for a small skiff to venture out far enough to find the right spot in deep water. This was a serious matter, for we needed fish to supplement our meager food supply. But this was the stormy season and there was nothing we could do about it without taking undue chances. In this part of the Port Chalmers area, there were no trout streams either.

We had found a large piece of heavy-gauge sheet iron near our first campsite, apparently from an old logging camp. This I now proceeded to make into a wood-burning heater and cookstove for our cabin. The only tools for the job were a hammer and a ¾-inch steel chisel. Some of the nails we still had were cut into rivets to hold the ends fast for the door. That was OK for getting wood into the stove, but taking ashes out was a problem without hinges. After some experimenting with slots and ears, two sticking in and one out, we had a functional door that also worked as a draft regulator.

The work on the 12-by-14-foot cabin was going along full speed. We planned a small cabin because a large one would take too much wood to heat. Before we even laid the foundation, though, we discovered that our part of the island was covered with a layer of peat bog and moss. The ground was soggy and wet, and where the floor was compacted in the tent, water would accumulate and stand. But we felt we had little or no choice—it might start snowing at any time and we were sick of the wet, crowded tent—so we proceeded with the cabin. In the middle of the floor, we dug a deep sump hole that we could bail out whenever it filled up.

Meanwhile, other activities continued. One day Sam explored as far north as Zaikof Bay, which we knew was there by our sketchy map. We estimated the distance as five or six miles and thought that some fine day we should all go look at some piling Sam had seen five miles or so out in the bay beyond where he had been. If this was a fish-trap location, we might find some food scraps or canned goods left by the trap watchman. And of course we still had wood to cut and ducks to hunt.

About our guns: Sam had a .22 from his Yukon days. Fred had a 12-gauge shotgun and I had a 300 Savage, brought with me from Unga. Sam's .22 and my Savage were in good condition. Fred's shotgun was a pump model with an exposed hammer, like the one on a six-shooter. To put it on safety, you had to pull the hammer back one notch off the firing pin. I had never seen one like it before and I never have since. Sam said the gun was unsafe because one day he had fanned the hammer and it had not stopped on the safety notch but had hit the firing pin. Luckily, the gun was empty. Fred and I didn't worry much about it, for we were used to handling guns.

One rainy afternoon, Fred returned from hunting ducks to find Sam and me in the tent having tea (Sam drank a lot of tea). As Fred took off his mackinaw, we kidded him for having fewer ducks than the shots he had fired. With no other place to put the mackinaw to dry, he hung it next to the stove on the barrel of the shotgun, with the stock on the ground. He leaned the gun against the roof of the tent, but he put a piece of wood between the tent and the coat so the rain-soaked tent wouldn't touch the coat.

Sam said, "Did you eject the shells?"

"No," said Fred. He did not like having the shells fall on the ground to get wet again.

"Well," Sam said, "that gun is unsafe. The shells should be out."

"Oh, hell," Fred muttered, reaching down and fanning the hammer. BANG! went the gun, and the chunk of wood disappeared through the roof of the tent.

It left a hole the size of a man's head in the tent and a three-inch hole through the collar of Fred's mackinaw.

Hunting mallard ducks was usually best at break of day and toward dusk. Some were migratory. Others would leave at daylight and return in the late afternoon to feed on small sea urchins and other creatures in the lagoon.

One day when I came home from hunting, Sam was outside the tent cutting wood and Fred was inside lying on the bed reading. As at our first camp, we had all the blankets and quilts laid out on the one bed. I didn't like to eject shells where they might fall on the ground and get wet any more than Fred did, so I stood next to the bed so the shells would fall on the blankets. The gun barrel was pointed two feet or so away from Fred when I ejected a couple of shells and BANG! The gun went off.

I can still see Sam with his ax in the air ready to chop a piece of wood. There was complete silence for what seemed a long time. Then from outside the tent came Sam's low voice: "Is he dead?"

Fred wasn't dead, but we had some big holes through all of our bedding.

Around the beginning of November the cabin was almost ready. The day all the roof poles were in place, snowflakes began to fall. We hurried to finish laying moss on top of the poles for insulation, but before the job was completed we had three to four inches of wet, heavy snow. We were so eager to get out of the tent and into the cabin, we tore down the tent, covered the cabin roof with the tent and a tarp, and moved in.

"BANG!" went the shotgun, and we had a hole the size of
a man's head in the roof of the tent

The proper way to keep this kind of roof from leaking is to be sure the tarp or tent cover is elevated, with a three- or four-inch air space between the moss insulation and the tarp. But the snow had caught us with our pants down and it was getting dark. The heat from the cabin would eventually dry the moss, we told ourselves, and we could elevate the tarp and tent come morning.

We hastily set up the stove and got a fire started. In a couple of hours the accumulated snow began to melt and drip. As best we could, we protected the bedding, personal belongings and groceries that had been moved in before we tore down the tent. Luckily we had enough oilskins and another tarp to cover most things, but we had only a candle for light. Every time a drop of water hit the candle, darkness would ensue. We moved the candle to various spots without success. By midnight the snowstorm outside had passed and the stars were out, but it was raining hard inside the cabin.

After sitting in the dark for a while—the inside of the cabin was now like a steambath—someone came up with the pregnant idea of putting a stick in the middle of the soggy peat floor beside the candle, and putting a wash basin upside down over the stick to make an umbrella. Now we could see a little through the steam.

We tried keeping ourselves dry by wearing raincoats, but this made us too wet and hot from steam and sweat, so we undressed and sat in our underwear until daylight. What a night!

In a couple of days we got things under control and began to feel dry, warm and comfortable. As time went by, however, our floor got wetter and wetter. Eventually we had to dig some cross-ditches running into the sump hole in the middle of the floor, which we bailed out morning and night.

Sam showed us a simple way to wash ourselves and keep our towels clean. By a slow-running brook, we each had a pole stuck in peat ground, and on those we placed our towels. Our soap was stuck on a separate pole. In the morning we would knock a hole in the ice, dip the frozen towel into the water enough to soften it, then

We finished the cabin just as the snow began.
Here it was Fred's turn to do some shoveling

wring it out thoroughly and wash and dry ourselves with the damp towel and hang it up again for the next time. It was invigorating and worked just fine.

One day the three of us made the trip north to check the fish-trap piling Sam had seen. We found nothing usable there. We each had taken along one cold hotcake and one unlabeled can of vegetables for our lunch. To my disappointment, when we opened our cans I had green peas. I had always hated peas—but I grew to appreciate them on Montague, and I've enjoyed them ever since.

It was a 20-mile round trip, so we were bushed when we got home. We had seen some signs of land otter, however, which was encouraging.

By this time, we had had to settle down to a regular routine. I spent most of my time duck-hunting. Fred and Sam did the cooking and wood-chopping. We were limited to a medium-size sourdough hotcake a day supplemented by one prune, three raisins and occasionally a can of vegetables. What little bacon we had was used for greasing the pan for hotcakes and for cooking ducks, which got skinnier and tasted fishier as time went on. For variation, we baked them, fried them, barbecued them, boiled them, but they always tasted fishy—more like lutefisk than the rib steak we craved.

Toward the end of November, a small powerboat happened to come into the lagoon and drop anchor for the night. The operator, a trapper from Cordova, told us we probably wouldn't get any otter until Christmas or after. He was short of groceries himself and couldn't spare any. We were not too worried, though, for our man was due any day. We were now out of practically everything but a little salt and those fishy ducks. Our stock of shells was also low, for as the supply of other food dwindled we had consumed more and more ducks. To top it all off, the Cordova man had a dog along with him that stole our precious bacon rind.

The agreed-upon day for our man to show up came and went, but he didn't arrive. Five days, 10 days, 15 days, almost a month went by. Still he didn't come. We were down to seven rifle shells, three shotgun shells—and none for the .22. Finally we began to feel desperate. We had six mallards left for food. Maybe something had happened to our man. He could have wrecked his boat or gotten sick. Maybe he was dead.

It was time for some tough decisions. We concluded that one of us would have to row the 10 miles of open water to Green Island, directly west of Port Chalmers. As we knew, Valdez Arm and Columbia Glacier to the north, not far from Green Island, have some nasty storms at that time of year, and so does the Gulf of Alaska to the south. The predominant winter winds hit Green Island from either the northwest or southeast. If those winds came up, fat chance of getting to shore!

I drew the short straw. It was going to be up to me. Although plenty apprehensive, I was glad too. I was stronger than Fred, and Sam couldn't row well.

Since the weather looked favorable, we lost no time getting ready. The skiff was in good condition, with a pair of oars and a good bailer. We made an extra pair of oars from some driftwood we had on hand, just in case one got lost overboard.

Before daylight on December 22, the tide being right for getting out of the lagoon, we were up and preparing for my departure. Sam and Fred were having second thoughts. If I didn't make it, they would slowly starve to death. If I did make it to Green Island and no one was there, I could probably survive on fox meat. They would still starve. It was a toss-up as to what was more dangerous: Stay behind or go with me. In the end we all three went.

This might seem foolhardy, but under no condition would one of us have volunteered to stay behind alone, although we knew that while two men rowing could make it with less effort to the other island, three would overload the skiff.

If we survived, we would be together. If we didn't, it would be the same.

We set out, taking with us some water and some roast mallards. There was a light wind from the west and a few snowflakes were falling. Sam was worried because we had to bail constantly and we had no compass. It was all right as long as we could see the island. If it began to snow harder, we would not know our directions. But we'd be OK as long as the wind was constant.

The wind and waves behaved but it was snowing hard by the time we reached land, about two in the afternoon. It had taken us five hours. Two miles an hour—good time, we thought. We ate our ducks on the beach after we landed. After that trip, they tasted like rib steak.

Where were the people, if any, living on the island?

We rowed two-thirds of the way around the island, or about 10 miles, before coming to a small cove with a boat at anchor. We had gone the wrong way but, thank God, we had made it.

By now it was dusk and snowing harder. Trudging from the cove we found a small house with a light. We knocked on the door and a man opened it. He was obviously surprised—he hadn't heard us coming.

But we were even more surprised, for against all the customs of the time he didn't ask us in. Through the partly open door we explained our predicament. He was not impressed. It took some time to convince him of our drastic plight. Finally, grudgingly, he let us come in and gave us some stew from a pot on the stove. Eventually he consented to letting just one of us stay with him until he made a trip to Latouche in four or five days. I was elected to stay.

To our complete consternation, he did not offer to let Sam and Fred spend the night. Being proud and tough, they were not about to beg him for anything, so after eating—we managed to empty the pot on the stove—they pulled out. The mean SOB did give them a loaf of bread and some dried salmon—fox feed, I guess—to take along. I followed them down to the skiff to wish them bon voyage. It was still snowing, and I almost cried watching them pull out in the dark.

They would spend the night in a collapsed old log cabin we had seen near where we had landed on reaching the island. Part of the roof was still off the ground and they figured they could build a fire alongside it. They promised to return if the weather got too bad.

The next day the snow had stopped and the wind was still light, so I felt pretty sure they had made it OK. I had eight dollars in my pocket, all we had among the three of us. I earned my board by helping to feed the foxes and, not trusting that grim-faced man, I slept with the rifle next to me and "one eye open." So passed Christmas 1925. On December 27, my unwilling host took me along on his trip

91

to Latouche and the next day I found a fisherman to go after Sam
and Fred.

Seven days after we had left Port Chalmers, the day before New
Year's Eve, the boat picked them up on Green Island and returned
to Latouche. I had already gotten a job in the mine and had been
lucky enough at blackjack to win more than $60, enough to pay off
the fisherman for the charter trip. A week later, Fred and Sam were
working, too.

Years later, I learned from Sam that he had been very concerned
about leaving me alone with a man who apparently had lost his
marbles. But Fred had reassured him: "I'm worried, yes, but not too
much. That 6-foot kid with a rifle can handle himself very well."
Even after all those years and all we had been through together I
was pleased to know of his confidence in me, for it had been a
frightening time.

The week on Green Island had been more miserable than dangerous for Sam and Fred. The first night they had rowed north in the
dark to where we first landed at the caved-in cabin. The snow by
that time was wet enough that they couldn't stay under the roof,
which was full of holes, so they built a fire under a big spruce tree.
In what was left of the cabin they found a couple of cans, one empty
and one loosely covered. In the covered can was some flour that was
still dry but had mouse droppings in it, which they carefully picked
out. Fred took the empty can to get some water from a nearby creek
and in so doing broke through the ice and got wet up to his knees.
After a dismal night, morning dawned fairly clear. They mixed the
flour and water and somehow baked it in the empty can. It kept
them going but Sam often said he had had better bannocks.

Fred learned later from a Dr. Council, a physician who practiced
in Cordova in 1925 and had stock in the Green Island Fox Corporation,
that when the company learned of our "welcome" on the island they

92

fired the man living there. They had already suspected that he was dealing in illegal furs.

And the fisherman who took us to Montague and was to pick us up? He had been found dead of appendicitis, and no one else knew where we were.

When my two daughters heard the story of our desperate crossing in the skiff from Montague to Green Island, they said, "Dad, now we understand why you always have a compass in your car!"

1.
Moonshine Business   101

2.
'Just Like Home on Montague'   107

3.
A Couple of Close Calls   113

[Confessions of an Alaska Bootlegger]

4.
Charlie's Big Mistake   121

5.
Was It 'Dead Sam's Camp'?   127

6.
Broke and Blue   131

7.
Honest Work   137

Foreword

It is not exactly true in our America that the two largest ethnic groups emigrating to these shores from Scandinavia have absolutely no use for one another. The alleged animosity is fictional. For example, I think it altogether unlikely that my Swedish ancestors referred in every instance to some Norwegian cousin as being "nothing but a Swede with his brains knocked out." That would be painting with much too broad a brush.

Evidence that we sons of Swedes and Norwegians can more or less get along together is found in my relationship with Ralph Soberg, a fairly nice fellow despite the fact he came from Norway, and will even admit to it.

Alaska, especially the southeastern coastal area, is full of transplanted Scandinavians who live happily along the fjords doing pretty much what their forebears did in the old country: fishing, mining, piloting small boats, and telling tall tales.

Soon after I moved to Juneau I became aware of a couple of fellow townsmen named Soberg. The truth is I knew the older brother, Fred, better than I did Ralph. As the plain-speaking editor of a small newspaper, I had a penchant for getting myself into trouble from time to time with some of the populace. Fred Soberg seemed to think about as I did on numerous subjects and often came to my defense. This was refreshing.

Ralph Soberg recently wrote a little book, *Survival on Montague Island*, about an Alaska adventure of his youth. I liked it and told him so. He has a nice way with words. Most of all he can make the real Alaska come to life on the printed page. Ralph told me he was writing another little book about an escapade in which he had been involved. This one was to be about Juneau. (The first had Prince William Sound as its locale.) Being misled into thinking I must know something about writing because I had been fortunate enough to have a couple of books published, he asked if I would look over the manuscript. This is that book, *Confessions of an Alaska Bootlegger*.

It is unlikely there was ever another town like Juneau. Although it was the capital city of an enormous territory, it had a population of considerably less than 10,000 at the time of which Ralph Soberg writes. What made Juneau unique was that it was connected overland with no other community whatever. There were a few miles of so-called highway, a gravel road which went nowhere except to its end, where the traveler could turn around and go back to town. The neighboring mining hamlet of Douglas was reached at that time only by boat across Gastineau Channel. The Juneau-Douglas bridge (which Ralph Soberg helped build) did not come along until years later.

Airlines did not then connect Juneau with the rest of the world, as they do today. The inaugural flights of Pan Am's clippers were not made until the early 1940s. Juneau was a little world to itself. It was served by one ship a week from Seattle and one Canadian ship from Vancouver, British Columbia. Small boats like Ralph's Magellan were necessary and numerous.

So there lay Juneau, surrounded by forest and mountains. The little city lived mainly on a large gold mine, in fact the largest lode gold operation in the United States, plus a little fishing, a sawmill, and a modestly staffed set of federal and territorial offices.

Juneau had one other thing—a thirst. Thereby hangs Ralph Soberg's tale. I commend it to you.

George Sundborg
Seattle, Washington
October 10, 1990

George Sundborg went to Alaska as a young newspaperman and remained to become the manager of the Alaska Development Board, executive assistant to the governor of Alaska, an elected delegate to the Alaska Constitutional Convention and, after statehood, administrative assistant to one of Alaska's two U.S. senators. He was editor of The Juneau Independent and later of the farthest north daily newspaper in the world, The Fairbanks Daily News-Miner. Books he has written include *Opportunity in Alaska* and *Hail Columbia,* both published by the Macmillan Company.

Alaska's capital city of Juneau lies on the mainland side of the Gastineau Channel. The large, terraced building on the mountain (right foreground) is the gold mill, with the Home Boarding House directly below. Far left is the Juneau-Douglas bridge, completed in 1935. The government dock, attached to Femmer's wharf, is the long white structure in the center (photo courtesy of Alaska State Library/Early Prints of Alaska collection)

Preface

Prohibition became the law of the nation in 1920, when the 18th Amendment to the Constitution went into effect. The Volstead Act of 1919 was passed to help enforce the new law. But supporters of the "dry" movement in Alaska had already succeeded in having liquor prohibited throughout the territory. In 1916, Alaskans voted 2 to 1 for prohibition, and The Alaska Bone Dry Law, passed by Congress in 1917, provided strict guidelines—stricter than those of the Volstead Act—for enforcing it.

I was on the wrong side of the law in the mid-1920s, part of a group of moonshine bootleggers in Southeastern Alaska. I could claim extenuating circumstances: I was young, and uneducated; I fell in with "bad companions"; times were hard; the law was often treated with little respect even by the people who were supposed to enforce it. All those things are true. But even then, I knew they didn't excuse me, and I'm grateful for the chance I eventually got to make a new life.

The 18th Amendment was repealed in 1933—an important year for me for other reasons—and Congress voided The Alaska Bone Dry Law in 1934. The glass of scotch I enjoy now in the evenings, when the sun is over the yardarm, is legal. Sköl!

Ralph Soberg

1.

Moonshine Business

Hard times sent my family from Norway to Alaska in 1919, and hard times sent my brother Fred and me from Hardscratch half a dozen years later, looking for work that would pay better than codfishing. For many people in the mid-1920s, the depression had already begun.

Fred, Sam Elstead and I were lucky enough to find jobs in the copper mine at Latouche after our escape from Montague Island. But I was young and had itchy feet, and in early 1926 I headed south to Juneau, the capital. Once again my experience growing up on boats in the Shumagins paid off—I got a job as an engineer on a cannery tender that summer. I hoped to get work in the Alaska Juneau Gold Mine for the winter, but no luck.

Had I not run into one of Fred's fishing friends, whom I had met in Latouche before the Montague expedition, perhaps I would not have gone astray. "Socks," so nicknamed because he washed his feet and his socks every day (which real fishermen just don't do), was staying on the 11th Street mud flats near the graveyard, out Willoughby

My brother Fred as a miner in Juneau

Avenue, where a French Canadian named Charlie Sinclair had some shacks for reasonable rent. I got a small room there for the winter.

Charlie had a power scow for hauling ice from Taku Glacier for Juneau Cold Storage, and I worked for him off and on that winter and also washed dishes in a restaurant. I didn't starve, but neither did I make money. I was now 18 years old and green as a hick can be, but full of self-confidence. It was a long, hard winter, however.

I soon learned that Charlie was Juneau's "king bootlegger." Sometime toward spring, 1927, Charlie approached me with a proposition. He asked me to make some moonshine sales to three or four of his regular customers while he was out of town on business—moonshine business, I assumed—in exchange for a free room plus a few extra bucks. He said the moonshine jugs were hidden under the boardwalk near my room. I mulled it over for a couple of days, then decided to do it but only for a short while. I realized later that Charlie was trying me out.

Who should arrive about that time but Sam Elstead, my Montague Island partner. He was trying to get into the gold mine, but he also had no luck. He moved in with me.

That summer, the U.S. marshals and Prohibition officers caught and arrested nearly all of the bootleggers in the area but the "Slippery Canuck" (Canadian), as Sam had nicknamed Charlie Sinclair. One day Charlie came to Sam and me with another proposition. He wanted Sam to be his moonshine cook and me to run his boat, the Magellan (named after the Strait of Magellan in South America).

Sam would get $2 per gallon to cook the brew, and I would get $1 per gallon for transporting it from camp to Juneau. Charlie already had a "salesman" working for him. It sounded like high adventure, and we didn't feel we could afford to be choosey, anyway, so we accepted. Things were getting tougher all the time.

The moonshine camp was located about 40 miles northwest of Juneau. It was on the mainland, across from Point Retreat on Admiralty Island, but could be reached only by water. That's where

"Socks" (far right) and friends. If I hadn't run into him, I probably would never
have become part of "the Slippery Four"

I came in. Charlie had been a fur trapper in the area, and he had
picked the spot because of its isolation and because the "Pro-Hi's"
(Prohibition officers), who were generally poor sailors, couldn't follow
him in the rough water that came up in the winter.

There are two ways to get to this area from Juneau. Large ships
are obliged to take a two- to three-hour run around Douglas Island,
but small boats like the Magellan can avoid this extra run of some
20 miles by proceeding almost as the crow flies northwestward up
Gastineau Channel between Douglas Island and the mainland. The
trouble with this route is that even a small boat can navigate it only
at high tide. The channel narrows and goes dry at low tide. With
care, the Magellan could make it through at high tide, as a meager
passage had been dredged through the tide flats. We had to be super

104

careful, however, as "crossing the bar," as it is described in Juneau, would take us past a perfect place for the Pro-Hi's to lay in wait for lawbreakers such as we. Fortunately, Charlie also owned an abandoned salmon cannery 10 to 12 miles north of Juneau at Auke Bay, where he stored supplies, including many empty charcoal kegs, acquired from who knows where. The cannery was a handy place to unload and tie up the boat if the time was wrong for crossing the bar.

The road to the old cannery was maintained by the Bureau of Public Roads and was cleared only to Auke Lake in the wintertime— about a mile short of Auke Bay—so we couldn't use it when there was much snow. Our route by boat from Auke Bay to the camp was in a westerly direction, through where the wind from the north in winter sometimes blows 50 miles an hour or more down Lynn Canal from Skagway and Haines. I knew my job as skipper would be demanding— ships have been sunk in the vicinity with all hands aboard.

Charlie's third man, "Rocky" George Johnsen, had earned his nickname working for the White Pass and Yukon Railroad on a rock-blasting crew. When he got laid off—probably because he never did care much for physical labor—he had bought several cases of Canadian bonded whiskey which he loaded on a small pump car he "borrowed" at the Canadian border north of Skagway to avoid U.S. Customs and the Pro-Hi's. He rode the pump car down to Skagway, where he had chartered a small boat to Juneau. The three of us were Charlie's entire crew, and if any of us were missing from town for a few days, the marshals and Pro-Hi's knew something was going on and got busy looking for us by sea and highway.

Sam, who was a practical joker, had nicknames for everyone. With Charlie, the Slippery Canuck, we were "the Slippery Four": George was "Slippery Rocky," I was the "Slippery Captain," and Sam was the "Slippery Danske" (Dane).

We each had our specific duties. My job was running the boat, Sam's was manufacturing the booze, Charlie was the manager, and Rocky, the retailer.

Rocky took care of the red light district along the waterfront. Among his customers were "Dolly Two-Shot," "Mary Broad Beam," "the Irish Dwarf," and "Three-Way Annie," a 60-year-old redhead.

I very seldom sold any booze, unless Charlie and Rocky were out of town. Sometimes I sold to a lawyer or law enforcement officer, and as a matter of fact, an assistant to the prosecuting attorney still owes me for two gallons of good moonshine.

2.

'Just Like Home On Montague'

Prohibition wasn't very popular in Juneau by the mid-1920s, but that fact—and even our having some of "the law" as customers—didn't mean we weren't in constant danger of arrest in a town of only 5,000-some people. But the Pro-Hi's were under-staffed and under-financed for the job they were expected to do, and we had some tricks for keeping a step ahead of them. For one thing, we made very few direct moonshine transactions. Charlie's usual system was to stash the jugs people had ordered in out-of-the-way spots for them to pick up themselves.

Even so, late that fall of 1927, Charlie decided the camp should be moved to a safer spot. He was afraid the Pro-Hi's were getting wise to the old location. Besides, he had several batches of moonshine already cooked and cached in charcoal kegs in various spots nearby for the usual three to six months of aging.

So, "the Slippery Four" took off for the old camp, anchoring the Magellan close to shore across from Point Retreat, up against a steep

Sam Elstead, my companion on Montague Island and again in Juneau

rocky incline. There was no harbor and nothing visible until we rowed ashore. A good stream ran through the rockpile, but it couldn't be seen from the waterway. The stills and mash barrels were about 50 feet back from the shoreline in the woods, completely hidden, and there was a makeshift sleeping shelter with a tarp over it.

Sam pointed this out and remarked to me, "Just like home on Montague, eh, Ralph?"

Charlie asked Sam and Rocky to start tearing down the camp and me to come with him. We pulled anchor and moved some distance north along the shore to a small cove. Charlie said it was a good harbor in case of one of the sudden storms that often hit the area. North of the cove, without disembarking, he indicated four different places where he had hidden five or six 10-gallon kegs for aging and future sale. He seemed to have a premonition that he was going to get caught eventually and would need someone he could trust to carry on for him so he would not lose his old customers. I was surprised that he had that much faith in me. In fact, I felt as if I was on the spot. This was the time I should have said no, but the thrill of the adventure still intrigued me. I said nothing.

(A month or two later I realized how shrewd he was. My God, I thought—I'm barely 19 years old and not a U.S. citizen yet. What will happen if I get caught running moonshine? Then I reasoned with myself. The offense would be a misdemeanor—but I had better stay away from smuggling scotch across the line from British Columbia, which would be a felony. If convicted of that, I would never get my citizenship papers.)

Before we left to join the others, I drew a rough map of the moonshine locations in case I had to pick up the booze by myself. When we got back, Sam and Rocky had the old camp torn down. We started loading.

The Magellan was a purse-seiner with a good-sized afterdeck. Most of the equipment, because of its bulk, went on deck. The stills, one 75-gallon, one 50, just barely went into the hold. The barrels and lumber went on deck. We covered everything with tarps so nothing would be apparent in case we met the Coast Guard or a U.S. marshal.

We three had no idea where Charlie intended to build the new camp, but he had picked the site months before.

We went back toward Juneau, then on down the south side of Douglas Island, through Stephens Passage south of Taku Harbor between Limestone Inlet and Snettisham Inlet, where we crawled up against the steep shore that came down the mountain and anchored at an old rock slide. It was about midnight and pitch dark. The weather was calm, so we put lines ashore and pulled the boat up against some rocks.

Again, there was a good stream of water running through the boulders. We unloaded everything as fast as we could and moved things into the woods, where we covered the lot with brush and willows. Then we pulled anchor and proceeded to a harbor in Snettisham where we slept until late the next day.

After the rest and some food, we upped anchor and went back to our new site, where I let Charlie, Sam and Rocky off to build the moonshine camp and Sam's "living quarters," if you could call it that. I went back to the harbor by myself to keep the Magellan out of sight until dark.

Near dusk I returned to camp with a pot of my good baked beans for supper, which we ate aboard the boat. Besides the beans I had fried an old, tough fishduck—like our Montague Island ducks—for Sam, to make him feel at home. By now the camp was nearly set up. Charlie was a good carpenter along with his other qualities.

After supper we finished setting up camp, connecting a water pipeline to the mash barrels and to the stills for cooling the coils. By midnight we were back at the anchorage. As we worked we had been constantly on the lookout for anyone who might spot us, for everyone in the country knew the Magellan and would know instantly what we were doing in the area. After a rest we headed for Juneau and home while it was still dark.

Dave Femmer, a good friend of ours, owned a large warehouse and wharf—a dock on piling—where we bought our supplies, including brown sugar, corn and corn meal for the moonshine. Attached to his pier, on the outside in deeper water, was the government dock, where the U.S. marshal and Prohibition boats were tied up. Inside

Rocky Johnsen, Sam Elstead and friend out Willoughby Avenue in Juneau

Femmer's warehouse was a hatch and a stepladder down to low tide, where at night we loaded the moonshine supplies into a skiff tied to the piling and rowed it to the Magellan. Charlie and I had keys for the back door so we could tie the skiff up at night and get ashore or row out to the boat. This was the safest area in town for lawbreakers —it was so close to the Coast Guard and Pro-Hi's that no one would be suspicious. However, for the protection of Dave Femmer, we never used it for transporting moonshine. We moved our supplies on the darkest nights, and when the "law" was busy and we felt it would be relatively safe. I was uneasy all the time, looking over my shoulder, and despite the sense of adventure that drew me on, that part was not pleasant at all.

On a dark night in September, we loaded up sugar and other supplies and took off for the new camp, Charlie, Sam and I. Rocky had a lot of thirsty customers to keep happy. I had made several trips to Charlie's old camp on Lynn Canal, so I was used to the procedure, but this was a new route and therefore more exciting.

We made sure the marshal's boat was tied up—for the night, we hoped—before our departure. Everything went fine.

The 25-mile run took more than two hours, still a lot less than the trip to the other camp. There were waves onto the beach, so it was difficult unloading from the Magellan and then onto shore, but this was the way it would probably always be. It was a matter of getting familiar with the procedure.

After the couple of hours it took to unload, I went alone to hide the boat in Snettisham Inlet for a day or two while Charlie helped Sam start all the mash barrels and try out the stills. None of us knew, when I picked up Charlie as per instructions and headed for home, that it would be a tough few months for Sam before he got back to Juneau.

3.

A Couple of Close Calls

As I said, the Pro-Hi's had pretty well cleaned out all of our competition in Juneau. Charlie upped the price of the moonshine to his customers, from $10 a gallon to $12, but continued to pay Sam and me only per our agreement.

With all those arrests in mind, I demanded that we equip the Magellan so I could drop and sink the moonshine kegs overboard in a hurry if I had to.

Charlie said, "You figure it out if you can."

So I did. I was always a good rigger and splicer, hence came my work on steel bridge construction later. I rigged up enough burlap bags with drawstrings to separately cover ten 10-gallon and ten 5-gallon kegs, and sinkers for each. The sinkers were made of small burlap bags with just enough sand in them to submerge the evidence. I began to experiment with 5- and 10-gallon kegs full of moonshine to make sure my plan worked, but I put the experiment aside when Rocky and I had to go back to the old camp for a load of moonshine.

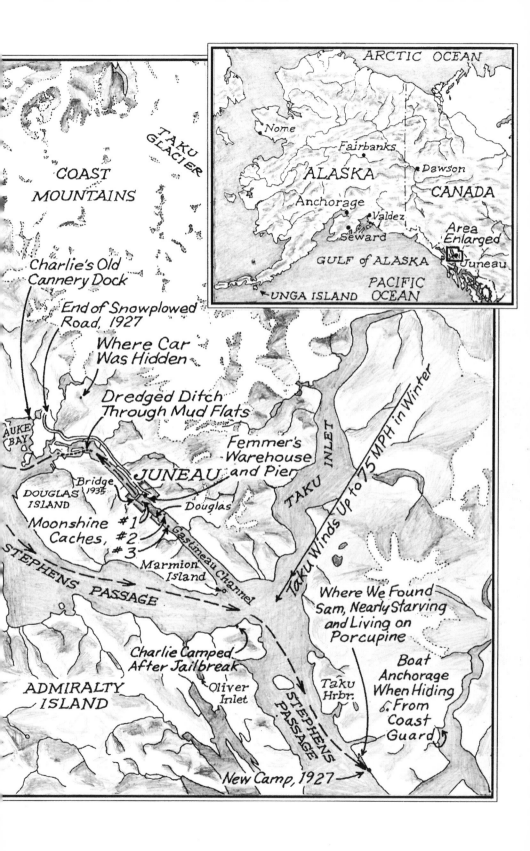

It was rough work, but the trip went smoothly enough. Loading 10-gallon kegs into a skiff is difficult, and loading them out of a skiff onto the deck of a boat is even more so, especially in a wind. Rocky could not carry a 10-gallon keg—they are awfully hard to get on your shoulder and hang onto after you do—so he carried the 5-gallon kegs. We cached most of the load north of Auke Bay (near where the ferry landing is now located), where Rocky and Charlie could get it by car and siphon some of it into 1-gallon jugs on the spot. That was the usual procedure. In the winter they would hide the jugs in the snow here and there near the city. They lost an occasional keg to poachers when tracks were hard to hide.

Our next trip on the Magellan was more difficult. We were returning from the old camp to Auke Bay on a moonless night at high tide so we could get over the bar between the mainland and Douglas Island. There had been no snow yet. Rocky was dubious that we could find our way without getting stuck on the mud flats, but I insisted we would be all right if I kept the boat at a low speed while he stayed on the bow with a pike pole and felt for the sides of the ditch. I had a feeling the Pro-Hi's didn't think we had the nerve to come over the bar, and I didn't think they had the nerve to fool around the mud flats at night, when they could get stuck for a couple of tides or more. We bumped a few spots going through, but each time we did, we backed off without any trouble.

We retested my emergency setup with the kegs when we got back to Juneau. Across from the Coast Guard dock on Douglas Island was a gradual sandy beach down to two or three fathoms that I thought would be ideal for our purposes. We anchored the Magellan around 2 in the morning. Conditions were perfect—it was calm and pitch dark—and we dumped the load as I had planned.

The kegs were arranged side by side in a half circle on the fantail stern of the Magellan, with a short tie between them so that if one was kicked over the side, the rest would automatically be pulled overboard like dominoes, with the sinkers attached. In our experiment, it took less than a minute for all of the evidence to disappear.

On the last keg we had tied a cotton rope heavy enough to sink, and to that a thin cord with a piece of driftwood the size of a large banana, just buoyant enough to float the string but not too noticeable.

We didn't worry about that good, aged moonshine being contaminated. The bungs on the kegs were hammered in tight and shellacked over so no salt water could enter. We had tested them before at 30 fathoms. If a load were ever dumped in a dangerous situation—which did eventually happen—we would gladly see it sink in a hurry and not be too selective about the depth of the water at the time. Of more importance would be to keep track of the approximate area and try to get a landmark so we could drag for the kegs when danger was past.

After the successful test, I relaxed and could breathe better, but I felt I was getting more and more alert. It seemed as if the wheels in my head had been oiled.

Now came another test of ingenuity. Was there a way to bottle the moonshine without hauling the kegs from place to place? The 10-gallon kegs were just too heavy and clumsy to get into the skiff without half swamping it.

We tried lashing a keg against the skiff as high as we could, to prevent seawater from splashing over the bung hole. I rigged up a small plunger pump with a thin hose on the intake end. This we inserted through a small hole we bored in the bung plug, which would be renewed when the keg was refilled. The pump outlet, of course, had a hose that went into the jug opening, and we always had enough of the glass 1-gallon jugs to empty each keg on which we were operating.

When the keg was empty, we let about a cup of sea water into it to ruin any dregs of evidence.

The operation worked well at the underwater cache where we first tried it, which we called No. 1 cache. Nos. 2 and 3 had to be transferred to No. 1 when all the kegs were empty, for No. 1 was

We used this old boat when we wanted to be inconspicuous

the only place we could get to with the skiff from behind the Coast Guard area.

The real test of my sinkers came late in the fall, on a freezing night with Taku winds from the north. The wind across the inlet was near gale force before I reached Point Bishop, coming in alone with a load. As I entered Gastineau Channel near Marmion Island, here was the Helmar, the U.S. marshal's boat, waiting for me. My heart jumped up into my throat for a bit, but I kept going near shore, where water would be shallow enough to dump the kegs without losing the load. It went just like clockwork. The marshals never saw me kick the load overboard, for it was near dark and I kept the boat heading enough their way that the pilot house shaded what I was doing on deck. A week later, Rocky and I dragged for the load, which we successfully retrieved and transferred to No. 1 cache near Douglas Island. The best part was, the Pro-Hi's didn't know for sure which way I had been coming that night—and they had the gall to search the boat after I landed!

I had another close call after a trip with Rocky on a boat we used for "emergency" runs, when we wanted to be inconspicuous. We came into town in broad daylight with several kegs of "sunshine," thinking that might throw the Pro-Hi's off. We unloaded in front of a children's home north of Juneau, past the graveyard, where Rocky stayed with the kegs while I returned the boat to the city float. After tying up, I noticed a quilt over something on deck. It was a full 5-gallon keg—and here I was, tied up only 50 feet from a Pro-Hi boat! I put the keg, quilt and all, under my arm and, with my heart pounding, sauntered as casually as I could past several people up to the Model T Ford I was driving, tossed the bundle into the car and headed through town to pick up Rocky and cache the load. Rocky said he had put the quilt on the keg for something soft to sit on.

After that I was glad for two uneventful trips alone to the new camp, which we now called Sam's Camp. Sam, of course, helped me load up.

Late in the fall, after a snowstorm, Charlie and I made a last trip to the old camp. I had to go around Douglas Island because of lack of tide high enough to float over the mud flats.

Charlie had driven a car to Auke Lake and had to walk the mile or so through the snow to his dock and warehouse, where I was waiting. We felt safe as far as the law was concerned. They didn't care for rough and freezing weather, and I sure didn't blame them.

We took off for the old camp, and as we approached Point Retreat, we saw salt spray ahead whirling 500 feet into the air. The wind was blowing at least 40 knots per hour from the northwest on our beam. We rolled like the dickens and iced up badly. I was glad to see how well the Magellan could take such conditions, for I knew the crossing of Taku Inlet could be much worse sometimes. We had a devil of a time locating all the moonshine and loading it, first onto the skiff, then onto the Magellan. As there was no danger from the law—no danger except maybe from sinking—we put everything in the hold and battened down the cover with a tarp. With this extra ballast, the boat behaved very well.

We got back to Auke Bay late the same evening and unloaded the cargo at the warehouse in secret places Charlie had concocted. From here on, I would be having no more to do with that batch. But Charlie said he just had to take a 5-gallon keg along for some of his gal friends, so we took turns packing it through the snow to his car at Auke Lake and returned to town about 3 a.m., cold and hungry. It had been a demanding but successful trip.

4.

Charlie's Big Mistake

We knew the U.S. marshals and Prohibition officers were on our tails, especially Slippery Charlie and Slippery Rocky. But now Charlie made a serious mistake. Without taking precautions, he set out on a Friday night in mid-November to deliver a gallon of hooch to a customer at the Home Boarding House, where many miners lived. The house was at the end of a one-way street, Gastineau Avenue, on the steep hillside above Juneau's main thoroughfare, back of several small rooming hotels on Main.

As Charlie stopped his car, a brand new Studebaker, he heard shots and spotted three men running toward him. He had been set up. There was no chance to turn the car around and get away, so he opened the door and kicked the jug, which was in a burlap bag, out onto the pavement. The jug broke as he intended, and the moonshine flowed away. But the bag was soaked. Ignoring a couple of acquaintances Charlie had picked up on the drive up the hill, the Pro-Hi's told him he was under arrest—but while they were busy

SINCLAIR, ACCUSED OF TAKING OWN CAR FROM DRY AGENTS, IS ARRESTED

Charged with purloining his own automobile, at least one owned nominally by him, Charles Sinclair was arrested Sunday by Federal authorities. Ralph Soberg, in whose room Sinclair was apprehended, was also arrested and charged with refusing to help the officers make the arrest.

The charge against Sinclair is an aftermath of his arrest last week on liquor charges. Federal Prohibition Agents Harding and Chidester Friday night are reported to have taken several shots at Sinclair's car while he was driving along Gastineau Avenue. Two passengers, according to Sinclair, were in the car at the time. Three bullets struck the machine. One of them, entering from the rear, passed through the back seat, and between the arm and body of one of the passengers, piercing his clothing but inflicting no wound, it was claimed.

The machine stopped near the Home Boarding House and the two agents, after searching the car and surrounding ground area, took possession of it. In the interim Sinclair had walked away while the officers were making their search. Later in the night Officer Harding drove the car, whi⸺ ⸺⸺⸺⸺er Stude⸺

SOBERG CHARGED WITH CONCEALING SINCLAIR

A charge of "unlawfully harboring and concealing a person from arrest" was filed yesterday by information in the Federal District Court by the United States Attorney's office against Ralph Soberg, operator of the Central Rooms. Bond was fixed at $1,500 by Judge T. M. Reed and was promptly furnished by the accused.

Soberg, it is charged in the complaint, concealed Charles Sinclair from Deputy Marshals Garster. Caswell, N⸺⸺⸺ ⸺⸺⸺ ⸺⸺

RALPH SOBERG CASE IS BEFORE COURT

The case of the United States vs. Ralph Soberg was opened in the U. S. District court this morning. Soberg is charged with concealing Charles Sinclair from the execution of a warrant for his arrest.

Three witnesses for the government were sworn in this morning, U. S. Commissioner Frank A. Boyle and deputy U. S. Marshals William Noble and Phil Herriman. It was expected the case would be ended this afternoon. H. L. Faulkner is counsel for the defence and U. S. District Attorney Justin W. Harding and Assistant U. S. District Attorney G. W. Folta are representing the government.

The members of the jury are: Henry A. Jenkins. ⸺⸺

---

wringing all of the evidence they could out of the burlap bag, Charlie calmly walked away and disappeared. Now he would have two charges against him—delivering moonshine and resisting or avoiding arrest. (Jack Diaz, one of his passengers, had had a close call: A Pro-Hi

122

bullet on its way through the car passed under Diaz' right arm, through his overcoat, sweater and shirt, but somehow didn't injure him.)

Until shortly before this happened, Rocky and I had been renting a room from a man by the name of John Paulsen, just below the Charles Goldstein Building. But Paulsen had asked me to stay at another flophouse he operated, almost directly below the Home Boarding House. In exchange for collecting for him from his renters— a sometimes unpleasant job, but otherwise not difficult—I had a nice big upstairs room, free. The going rate was 50 cents a day ($1 and up in places with running water).

A couple of days after the Pro-Hi's tried to arrest him, Charlie walked in on me through the back door on the second floor, which was level with the hillside in back of the building. He told me what had happened and asked me to take over his whole operation until things calmed down. We had no more than completed that discussion when the U.S. marshals arrived through the same door. They had been on Charlie's tail since he strolled away from them. They arrested us both—Charlie for transporting moonshine and me for concealing a person from arrest. This was about 2 p.m. By 5 p.m., our lawyer, H.L. "Bert" Faulkner, had us out on bail. Faulkner said for us to lay low for a while and he would try to speed up a possible trial, which he did.

In the meantime, Charlie came back to my room to complain: "The damn Pro-Hi's are using my car for running around town! That's not legal before the court takes the title away—and that won't happen unless I'm convicted."

"Right now they're having a party at so-and-so's," he said, "and the car is sitting on the street in front of the house. I've got a spare key. What do you say we borrow it from them and drive to Mendenhall Glacier and hide it for a while?"

Not having learned a thing from the trouble we were already in, I said, "OK. Let's go."

Charlie was driving the Model T. He dropped me off right in

Sam Elstead and I—the moonshine "cook" and the "captain" —near Switzer's
Dairy, about halfway to Auke Bay from Juneau

front of the house, next to the Studebaker, and I just stepped right into it—the doors were not even locked. The car started immediately, and I headed out Glacier Highway, as we had arranged. About two miles from the glacier, I stopped for Charlie, and he picked a place to hide the "hot" car.

I drove it off the road through some brush as far as I could until it was completely hidden by high alder and willows. All we had to do was cover our tracks as well as we could and hope for some quick snow. Around the glacier that didn't take long, and the car wasn't found until spring, six months later.

An officer later testified that he saw Charlie take the car from in front of the house where it was parked, but he was mistaken (or worse).

JACK MITCHELL HELD HERE AS SINCLAIR AID

Marshal White Says He Is Man Who Sawed Hole in Local Federal Jail

Interest in the celebrated Charles Sinclair case was revived today with the announcement by U.S. Marshal Albert White of the arrest of Jack Mitchell on a charge of aiding and abetting Sinclair's escape from the local Federal jail on or about April 23 last. The warrant was issued on a complaint signed by Deputy Marshal W.E. Feero.

Mitchell is alleged to have sawed a hole in the jail through which the escape was made. It was 9 by 17 inches in the inner side and 7 by 13 inches in the outer bars. He was recently brought here to complete a jail sentence imposed in Skagway.

Other prisoners incarcerated in the local jail are said by Marshal White to have been implicated in the delivery at least to the extent of making an (un)usual amount of noise while the hole was being sawed in the walls and bars of the tank and while Sinclair made his get-away.

In November 1927, Sinclair was arrested (and) charged with bootlegging, after two Federal Prohibition agents had fired three shots into a car in which he and two others were riding down a blind street. One of the bullets passed through the coat of one of the men in the car. The auto was taken by the officers and later on the same day was taken away from before the residence of one of the officers who testified he saw Sinclair take the machine.

Sinclair was convicted on December 14, 1927, and was sentenced to two years imprisonment in the local Federal jail and to pay a fine of $1,500. He served about four and one-half months of the term, becoming a model prisoner, according to Marshal White. He was permitted to see a number of visitors and transact business for the disposal of certain property interests. On April 23, this year, when his attorney called to see him, the prisoner could not be found, and a checkup disclosed the escape and the holes in the jail.

Sinclair in his hurried departure left behind him a good photograph of himself. Copies were made of it and scattered broadcast all over the country and even to Great Britain.

Rumors from time to time came to officers of Sinclair's presence in various places and posses were sent out several times on unsuccessful searches.

The first definite word of the fugitive came from Port Althorp. Investigation showed that a man corresponding to his general description had been there on a small boat and bought some supplies. No further trace was uncovered in that direction.

In the early part of August, an individual whose name was not revealed by Marshal White and who refused to take any part of the reward money offered, gave the Marshal Sinclair's post office address at Prince Rupert. He was arrested there on August 14.

Efforts to have him deported failed, but Ottawa authorities ordered him released and given 90 days to leave Canada. However, representations made by local Federal authorities resulted in his detention by Prince Rupert police pending the outcome of extradition proceedings.

The matter of extradition is now the subject of diplomatic negotiations between the United States Department of State and the Ottawa Government.

Coincident with Mitchell's return here to be tried on the charge of aiding Sinclair escape, Marshal White issued a statement reviewing his work on the case.

"I gave much time and thought to working out this case, trying to apprehend Sinclair and fix the responsibility on those who aided in his escape," he declared. "My 10 years' experience in the Department of Justice, including work in large cities such as New York, Chicago, San Francisco, Denver and Seattle, equipped me with knowledge valuable in solving the case.

"Graduating under the direction of William Burns, and attending Government schools Chicago and New York, I have found that the criminal can be caught in Alaska as elsewhere."

Referring to his success in handling prison since taking office, the Marshal said, "I feel a pride in the fact that in 28 months, when handling about 100 prisoners daily in the jails of the First Division there has been only one escape. This was Sinclair and he was recaptured after three months of liberty

speak f...

5.

Was It 'Dead Sam's Camp'?

I was getting worried about Sam. The last time I'd seen him, I had promised to come pick him and the last kegs up in a week. That had now been more than 10 days ago, but after the warning from Faulkner to lay low, and with all the stink over the disappearance of Charlie's car, I was told to stay in port, period. Our trial in the U.S. District Court was on the docket in another week or so, and Charlie and I had several meetings in Mr. Faulkner's office for pre-trial guidance.

Faulkner said I had a good chance for acquittal because I had not really hidden Charlie from arrest and because I was under 21. He told me he would pick churchgoing people to be on the jury because they would tend to be more sympathetic to a "nice, clean young man" like me.

Charlie's case was something else. After all the years he had been in the moonshine business, we would just have to hope for the best.

My trial took two days, and I went free. The jury was out for only four hours, and acquittal was unanimous on the first ballot. Yes, Mr. Faulkner did succeed in having mostly church people on the jury!

Now Charlie had a premonition of a guilty verdict. He asked me to move into his house and take charge if he were convicted and jailed immediately. He told me where all his caches were and gave me details of other important matters.

He didn't think, though, that he would get more than a short sentence. But he was convicted on four counts—resisting officers, possessing and transporting moonshine, and destroying evidence—and besides being fined $1,500 was sentenced to three years in the federal jail, two of them to run concurrently. We had no chance to talk again without a guard overhearing.

It was now around six weeks since I had left Sam. I was at a loss as to what to do. Poor Sam. He would be out of food by now. But I was scared to make a move, and Rocky was, too. We waited for another couple of weeks, until we thought we could wait no longer or Sam would starve to death.

On a stormy night we sneaked out on the Magellan from the city float. Taku Inlet was rough, and we iced up a lot, but the Taku wind didn't reach down to Sam's camp—or was it "dead Sam's camp"? We felt safe as far as the law was concerned. They would never take on the Taku Inlet in this kind of weather.

We swung in close to the camp and yelled for Sam. No answer. We decided to go anchor at Snettisham until daylight, then go back to see what we could find. In the morning we upped anchor and went back to search.

Everything looked strange because of the new heavy snow. We anchored close to shore where the camp should be and rowed the skiff in. I waded through hip-deep snow to where our things had been, but nothing could be seen. Sam had apparently covered every-thing with brush and spruce boughs. His shelter, such as it had been, was completely gone—no evidence that it had ever been there.

Knowing Sam as I did, and trying to put myself in his place, I decided he must have figured that the Pro-Hi's had nabbed us and that we were all in jail, so he cached everything in case they came snooping around his area, and then he moved to a safer place to wait it out.

From habit, I hated to be anchored very long at our place of illegal manufacturing. We moved away toward where I thought Sam would most likely be if he were still alive, about half a mile north toward Taku Harbor. We anchored and rowed the skiff back along the shore to what we thought was a likely area. Rocky stayed with the skiff, and I slogged through the deep snow to several different spots.

It was beginning to get dark again—short days this time of year—and I saw nothing. But at one place, after I had yelled several times, I heard something! My heart almost stopped. I yelled again and held my breath. My God, it was Sam. I spotted a faint flash of light and waded as fast as I could through the snow toward it.

Sam said, in a low, weak voice, "Is that you, Ralph?" After hearing me call his name, he had lit a match, and this is what I had seen through a canvas cover he had over his makeshift abode. He had kept it clear of snow to keep it from caving in and to let in some daylight. The canvas formed a kind of cave in a rockpile, where a sliver of water was trickling down from the mountainside. He hadn't had to leave his shelter except for bathroom purposes—and to knock a porcupine over the head for meat. He had brought some kerosene and a burner from the stills for warmth and cooking.

Sam had lost a lot of weight, and he told me he didn't like porcupine meat any better than our Montague eider ducks. Other-wise, he was OK. He was sure glad to see me, and he had not lost his sense of humor. We wasted no time getting him on board the Magellan and heading for home. Of course we fed him, what he

Sam, here on 11th Street, looked pretty rough when we got him
back to Juneau after his ordeal at the moonshine camp

called "strange, but good" food.

A month later we returned to the camp site and cleaned out all evidence of any illegal activities. We took everything and stored it at the Auke Bay warehouse, except for the moonshine, which we cached for future business.

130

6.

Broke and Blue

Now Rocky and I had a reputation, a rather infamous one. We were the only suspected culprits who had not been caught, and we had no competition. But we were too scared to take advantage of this, so we laid low.

One evening a taxi driver came to me at Charlie's place, where I was living, to say that Dolly Two-Shot was desperate for a gallon of the good stuff for her customers but that Rocky was too scared (I think he meant too sensible) to supply it. I told him to wait there.

I took the old Model T and headed north a mile or so on the highway past the graveyard, where a little trail went up to the mountain. I stopped the car at the trail and ran quickly up the path and grabbed a gallon jug that was hidden under a root. This took only a minute or less. As I turned to head back, I saw someone going through the car with a flashlight. Of course I knew immediately what was happening.

I heard a man say, "The radiator is still warm. He can't be far away." The night was crisp and calm, with no snow, just a little frost. I turned and bolted up the path in the dark. As I ran, I held one arm in front of my eyes to keep from getting hit by the brush. Voices yelled at me to "stop or we'll shoot," which they soon did. I heard bullets hit some branches, but I never stopped. Nor did I let go of the jug. Had I done so, they would have had the evidence they needed. I swung into the graveyard and hid for a while among the gravestones—long enough to decide that if I got out of this scrape I would reconsider my line of work. When I thought it was safe, I walked home and hid the jug, then retrieved the car and delivered the moonshine. That, I told myself, was that. Or would be, as soon as we got rid of the last of Charlie's cached kegs.

At about that time, three months or so after Charlie went to jail, Jack Diaz came to the house to tell me that Charlie wanted a pair of slippers. Not just any slippers, he said. I was to get "the Tarheel," a hardware store operator named Frank Harris, to glue a hacksaw blade in each slipper, and Diaz would deliver the slippers to Charlie in jail. When Charlie decided on a day and time for breaking out, the Tarheel was to have a skiff loaded with camping gear tied up under the warehouse.

As soon as I got word of the proposed jail-break date, I made plans to be gone from town a couple of days before. I took Rocky with me to Excursion Inlet and tied up at a cannery so we would have an ironclad alibi.

A week later we returned to Juneau, escorted by the U.S. marshals. They arrested me, but not Rocky, and charged me with aiding and abetting Charlie's escape. I was bound over to the grand jury for investigation and put on $1,500 property bond. Mrs. Burford, who owned a grocery store, went my bond, which I was on for two years, until the grand jury returned no true bill on me. The government confiscated all of Charlie Sinclair's property, boat and house included, so I had to find another place to live.

At the marshal's sale, I talked a fisherman acquaintance of mine named Ronning into buying the Magellan, and we rigged it up for trolling salmon near Sitka that summer. Fishing was no good, so we and several other boats did some illegal creek fishing in Kelp Bay and nearly got caught when the fish warden unexpectedly appeared. The crews of 14 boats were arrested, but the Magellan and two other boats escaped through a kelp bed and between some rocks. We sailed into a storm and had to go into a harbor for which we had no chart. The entrance had strange Kootchnahoo Inlet currents. We hit a rock and the Magellan sank—a complete loss. Finally I was convinced that crime doesn't pay!

Ronning left me with the boat on the rocks. Without help I could do nothing but leave it where it was. He took most of the valuable gear—lead sinkers and brass trolling spoons, etc.—and left

The Magellan's grave, about 100 miles south of Juneau

me with more than $500 in bills in Juneau. Later, too late, I found out he was known more as a pool shark and gambler than as a fisherman. More education for me.

When I returned to Juneau, I was pretty blue. By the time the bills were all paid, I was broke and disgusted and decided it was time to go straight.

I went up to the courthouse to see the assistant U.S. attorney, George Folta, who had been the prosecutor on my trial. I asked him point-blank whether, if I applied for citizenship papers, they would turn me down.

He smiled and said, "Well, we know you've been associated with some shady people. But you haven't been caught or convicted of anything. If the grand jury doesn't bind you over for trial over Sinclair's jail-break, we can't legally say no, provided you pass the citizenship examination."

While I was trying to decide what to do with myself—Folta had said I needed five years of good conduct before I could start the citizenship process—a fisherman came to me with a note from Charlie Sinclair. He wanted the Tarheel to pack some groceries and clothes for me to bring to him east of Oliver Inlet. He knew I would guess pretty close where to find him. A skiff with an outboard would be the safest way to get there.

The Tarheel and I took off on a clear, sunny day. When we got close to the beach where I thought Charlie would be, we yelled for him and he came out of the woods, looking awfully rough, with long whiskers and torn clothes. He told us he was going to row to Canada, a distance of some 400 miles down the coast. The note he had sent for the Tarheel had listed everything he would need for the trip, including a mast and sail for his skiff. The Slippery Canuck was a naturalized U.S. citizen, but that wasn't going to stop him.

We said our good-byes, and that's the last I ever saw of Charlie Sinclair. Before we left him, he told me where to find some kegs of moonshine to pay the Tarheel, which I did. The Slippery Four were

I slept under a tarp for 10 nights at this village near Killisnoo,
after the Magellan hit the rocks

now officially disbanded. Sam was working in the gold mine, and
Rocky was selling what was left of the moonshine on his own.

As for me, with high hopes I borrowed a hundred dollars from
one of the George brothers and bought a ticket to Seattle in early
December 1928.

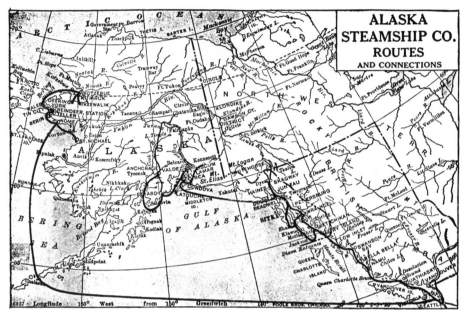

MINIMUM PASSENGER FARES

The passenger fares shown below are the steamer fares in effect January 1, 1929, covering minimum ordinary accommodations on steamers named, from Seattle to the ports named when steamers operate to such ports. Rates include berth and meals, except that on steerage tickets, which are sold only to men, steerage passengers must furnish their own blankets.

From SEATTLE To	First-Class—Upper Deck Ordinary Accommodations		First-Class—Saloon Deck Ordinary Accommodations		Steerage Men Only	Children's Fares (See Page 21)	Distances from Seattle	
	One Way	Round Trip	One Way	Round Trip	One Way	One Way	Miles	Days
Ketchikan	$34.00	$68.00	$30.00	$60.00	$17.00	$5.00	757	2
Wrangell	39.00	78.00	34.50	69.00	19.50	5.75	859	3
Petersburg	41.00	82.00	36.00	72.00	20.50	6.00	907	3
Juneau	46.00	92.00	41.00	82.00	23.00	6.85	1,033	3-4
Haines	50.00	100.00	45.00	90.00	25.50	7.50	1,137	4-5
Skagway	50.00	100.00	45.00	90.00	26.00	7.50	1,153	4-5
Sitka	50.00	100.00	45.00	90.00	26.00	7.50	1,335	5-6
Cordova	74.00	148.00	66.00	132.00	37.00	11.00	1,599	5-6
Valdez	75.00	150.00	67.00	134.00	37.50	11.15	1,686	6-7
Latouche	75.00	150.00	67.00	134.00	37.50	11.15	1,783	6-7
Seward	78.00	156.00	70.00	140.00	39.00	11.65	1,856	7
*Nome	115.00	230.00	85.00	170.00	50.00	15.00	2,500	9-10
*St. Michael	115.00	230.00	85.00	170.00	50.00	15.00	2,620	9-10

*No service during winter. Fares applicable only during open season of navigation.
For rooms with bath fares are from 25% to 40% higher than upper deck fares quoted herein. Fares for any particular room furnished on request.

For additional information regarding our service to Alaska, both freight and passenger, address

ALASKA STEAMSHIP COMPANY
Pier Two, Seattle, Washington
L. W. BAKER, General Freight and Passenger Agent

H. N. PETERSON, Assistant General Passenger Agent   J. D. NELSON, Assistant General Freight Agent

Seattle City Ticket Office, 1401 Fourth Ave., Corner Union St.   San Francisco City Ticket Office, 683 Market St.
Los Angeles City Ticket Office, 519-20 Foreman Bldg., 707 South Hill St.

WHEN YOU THINK ALASKA, THINK ALASKA STEAMSHIP COMPANY

PRINTED IN U.S.A.   © ALASKA STEAMSHIP COMPANY, 1929   23   27893 POOLE BROS INC., CHICAGO

7.

Honest Work

Jobs were harder and harder to find, but by Christmas I was working as a deckhand on a Foss tugboat, Foss #18, towing logs from Sidney, B.C., to the Ballard Locks and moving barges here and there. At the end of March, when the weather started to be nice, I wanted to be in town more. I quit the tugboat job and went to work for the Cascade Lumber Company, rafting logs in Tacoma, where my mother, my brother Egil, and my sister, Ida, were now living. I worked this job until September 1929, when my brother Fred came down from the Port Althrop cannery.

Fred suggested we go to Seattle and enroll at Edison Technical School. I quit my job, and we moved up near the school. But things were too expensive. In October we shipped out to Mexico on the Ruth Alexander, a passenger liner that was later torpedoed by the Japanese during World War II. We first had to get our lifeboat tickets from the Coast Guard. I went on as a wiper, cleaning up the engine

Mother in Juneau about 1940

room, and Fred as an ordinary seaman. Before we got to San Francisco, I was an oiler, and I got my oiler's ticket on landing back in Seattle.

In December 1929, as short of cash as ever, Fred and I decided to stow away on a passenger ship to Alaska. We made it aboard with our gear just fine, around 3 in the afternoon. But we went ashore again when we found out the ship wasn't sailing until 10 p.m., and getting back on board we were caught.

Since our stuff was on the ship, one of us had to go, somehow. Between us we had enough money for one steerage ticket, so we flipped a coin and Fred won. I hitched a ride to Tacoma, borrowed

My sister, Ida, and her baby, and my brother Egil, in Juneau

$25 from Mother, and caught the next ship north.

When I got to Juneau, Fred had a job in the mine. I did odd jobs, so we were OK over the winter.

The next year, I fished with Rocky—no longer "Slippery Rocky" —on his gillnetter at Haines and went to night school to study for my citizenship papers. My five years of good conduct were up in 1933. I appeared before Folta, and he gave me a stiff grilling, for which I did not blame him. He almost stuck me when he asked me to give an example of the difference between federal and state government authority and law. I think I missed it a bit, but he recommended I get the papers. He was really a fine man.

Becoming a citizen was a big relief. But I was rogue enough to wonder whether I'd have had all this fun and adventure—for such it seemed now that I was through with it—if I had gotten the education I'd always resented missing out on after we left Norway. Then my thoughts turned more serious. I had often had occasion to remember my mother telling about my deciding to be born while

"Squeaky" Anderson (right)—later a U.S. Navy admiral—and one
of his crew members on the iced-up Starr

140

First mate Chris Hansen (left) and Captain Christen Trondsen,
when Chris Trondsen was skipper of the Starr

she was milking the cows. Now it occurred to me, without disrespect:
Like Jesus, I was born in a manger. He was nailed to the cross for
being a good person. How is it I went free for being a scoundrel?

A citizen, even a newly upright citizen, still had to find work.
In May 1933, I went to Bristol Bay on the SS Starr, which in the
early years on Unga Island had been our lifeline to the rest of the

141

A friend, Curly Davis (right), and I skinnydipping on Admiralty Island in 1931. We were brave to be swimming—the woods around the lake were full of brown bear

world. Chris Trondsen, who later skippered the Starr and has been a lifelong friend, was first mate on that trip, and Chris Hansen, another longtime acquaintance, was first engineer. I fished at Dillingham and then went home to Hardscratch, where I ran my uncle's boat and fished for salmon, which we salted in barrels. We lost money on that venture. The price at Bristol Bay that year was 6 cents per fish. In 1989 the average was $9 per fish.

I returned to Seattle later in 1933 as engineer on a power barge with Admiral "Squeaky" Anderson, a famous commander in the Aleutian Islands during World War II. With us was Harold Lauritzen, my future wife's brother, with whom I roomed in Seattle for a month.

I shipped out again with Squeaky on his trading schooner Polar Bear for the Aleutians, but by the time we reached Petersburg, the thought of a winter out in the islands made me change my mind

142

and I quit, returning to Juneau where by now my mother, my sister and all of my brothers lived.

In 1934, I got work as a diver and rigger-crane operator for Dishaw Construction Company on the Juneau-Douglas bridge. Here I found my niche at last! I loved bridge work. I went on to spend many years on bridge and road construction all over Alaska under a fine mentor, A.F. "Gil" Ghiglione, who was bridge engineer and eventually chief engineer for the Alaska Road Commission and, after statehood, chief engineer for the Bureau of Public Roads out of Juneau before he was transferred to Washington, D.C., to oversee international projects.

But that, as I once said about the bootlegging escapade, is another story.

Ralph Soberg, 1935

Fred Soberg, 1925

Epilog

Sixty years and many adventures after we rowed away from Montague Island, my brother Fred, "the Professor," was fatally injured when he was struck by a car on his way to mail a letter to the editor of the newspaper in Sitka, where he was living at the Pioneer Home. He had shortly before made a trip around the world. A few years before that, he had been back to Norway with me, and then to Greece, Spain, Russia and China.

Sam Elstead, our partner on Montague Island and my fellow bootlegger, died in Denmark in 1965.

Brother Ed stayed with Mother after Dad died, until 1929, when they all—Mother, Ed, Ida and Egil—went out to Tacoma on a cannery tender. Ed eventually joined Fred at the gold mine in Juneau (I had been blacklisted at the mine because of my teenage bootlegging career), and Mother, Ida and Egil moved to Juneau, too.

When Fred and I got steady work with the Alaska Road Commission, we were able to help Mother. Egil, who had always been frail, became ill with tuberculosis in the '30s, and Fred and I sent him to Arizona for treatment. He died there. I don't know where he's buried.

Sister Ida married a man in Juneau during the Second World War and went Outside, as Alaskans call the lower 48 states, with him and their baby. Fred got a telegram from her asking him to wire $50. Three or four days later, the money came back. We never heard from her again.

Ed died during the war, working for the Navy. He is buried in Sitka, and Mother in Juneau, where she died in 1957. Sorting through the things stored in the attic of her little house, I found Egil's old 4-string banjo, which she had put away 20 years before when he went to Arizona.

Uncle Nick—Captain Hardscratch—stayed on the island by himself after Mother left. He died in 1939 at Soap Lake, Washington.

For years after leaving Hardscratch, always eager and impatient for whatever was coming next, I didn't look back. But it's clear to me now that there is no escaping our beginnings.

In the village of Unga, where Ida and Egil boarded and went to school, things probably would have been better for us. But we older boys were just at the age where we could begin to handle a man's job, and we were needed. So, we occupied ourselves at Hardscratch as best we could.

But my lonesomeness there is undescribable now. As I began to grow up, all women, young and old, looked good to me. There were none my age north of Squaw Harbor. My company was my good imagination.

If I saw a steamer, maybe the Catherine D., coming around Popof Head, I would take off running from the farm to Squaw Harbor, about six miles, and beat the ship before it got tied up.

Or if a dance was to be at Sand Point, I would push the power dory off the beach alone (a power dory weighed at least 1,500 pounds)—I'd lay skids under the boat and push it, one end a little, then the other, until my breath was all gone. Nothing was impossible. I was so full of energy.

References

As Ralph Soberg says in *Captain Hardscratch and Others*, his fisherman-musician father, John Johannessen, directed a men's choral group in Norway and wrote some of the songs the group sang. Ralph had a copy of the following song, written in dialect and printed in an unknown publication. Glenn Eriksen of the *Seattle Post-Intelligencer* has kindly translated part of it:

"*Mandsangforeningen* 'Heimklang' is basically 'Men's song club *Heimklang.*' (Melody: The Norwegian Valley Song, by Petter Dass.) 'Heimklang' would roughly translate to 'Sound of Home,' or 'Music of Home.' The first five lines of the song go something like this:

'The men's song club *Heimklang* struggled so faithfully
    with its choral singing.
Whenever the opportunity availed itself, they would practice.
On Sundays and workdays, they would gather from all corners,
Søberg, Skårvågshag;
Forøy, Straume, Børje and Vea, fishermen and people who
    sew clothes.'

"Then the song employs nautical analogies—the choral instructor is the captain of the ship; he gives the order and the chorus (crew) haul in the anchor and set off to sea (start singing). The song goes on to mention names of some in the club, drawing analogies between their actual roles or jobs aboard ships and their parts in the chorus. An example:

'Henrik's foghorn (bass?) was as clear as a church bell.
Sigurd Søberg jumped on the pump.'

"The song proceeds in this manner and closes by paying tribute to a song club member who has died in a storm at sea:

'Julius and his brother and his father have found their graves
    on the bottom of the sea.'"

MANDSANGFORENINGEN «HEIMKLANG»

Mel.: «Den nordske Dale-viise» av Petter Dass.

Mandsangforeningen Heimklang bala så trutt med sin korsang.
Kvar en gong det høv seg, de øv seg.
Synn- og arbeidsdag samles de i lag ifra kvert et snag,
Søberg, Skårvågshag',
Forøy, Straume, Børje og Vea, feskarfolk og folk som syr klea.
Først får eg nemn instruktøren: taktslagan slår han med klørn'
– gaffelen i bore åt kore –
og så tin de opp; d'e med hei og hopp de hiv ankret opp
på kommandorop,
og så held de sakte utover, sjøl i rokk og hemlanes skavêr.
Julius Børje og Reinholdt, folk som braut på, mean bein holdt.
Så kom Johan på Vea, de mea:
Petter'n styr så kløkt, manøvrer så snøgt at de føl kje frøkt,
båten ligg så trøgt
at de slepp å ta han på åran, vinden kasta om med de står han.
Henrik sin tåkelur verka klårt ness som klokka i kjerka.
Sigurd Søberg jumpa på pumpa.
Reidar Engenes, han e alle steds, spreng i sjy te knes
om så høve gjes.
Sigurd Små-ås grev i lugaren: han e kokk på skuta, den karen.

Albert på andre-tenoren bryt, og han John i motoren
skruva, smørr og perka og lerka.
Halvdan Forøy fér riggen opp og ner sjøl i verste ver
som Vårherre gjer.
John på Øyjord passa på piken. Jørgen Vea skjerpa øyrfiken.

Jakobsen, Heimklang-solisten, skade at laget sku mist'n:
Når en slik en sprek, gasta kar gikk vekk, då blei skuta lekk.
Heimklang fikk en knekk
så det stakkars skrove blei gresse: Pumpa gjør de stadig og stedse.

Men eg har glømt nå'n strika, nemlig han Søren i Vika.
Ham e e gjæv på basen, den nasen.
Og på Gjemsta har vi han Både-far, d'e en gasta kar:
Tvila mange har
hér i Bø og Malnes en bass-stemm' djup og klar og rein liksom hass stemm'.

Heimklang har en som vi sakna. Etter en storm då det spakna
kom det bu fra Vågen, de såg en
firroringsbåt nyss va dreven åt mella fall og brott.
Der blei sorg og gråt:
Julius og broren og faren fann si grav der ute i taren.

Jon Johannessen, Søberg

Ole Søberg.

I. Johan Johannesen, f. på Hole 1834, d. 1901, s. til Johs. Olsen.
Med kona fekk han halve Øverjorda. Han kjøpte gardpartar kring i bygda,
såleis i Skårvågen og Vågen.
G. 1854 enka Elen Maria Matiasdtr. Mørk, f. på Strønstad i Hadsel 1824.
Ho var før g. m. Hans Nilsen, som sette til i 1850. Elen d. i 1915.
Barn:

II. 1. Helene Maria J., f. 1854, g. Lars Robertsen, Skårvågen.

II. 2. Nikoline Martine J., f. 1857, d. 1940, g. 1877 Mons Monsen. Kom til
Bø i 1876. Kjøpte i 1895 Elverhøy, 39/14. I herredst. 1914—16.
Barn:

III. 1. Amalia Nikoline M., f. 1878, g. Helmer Andreassen, Søberg.

III. 2. Matilde Marie M., f. 1880, g. Aslak Hansen, Ringstad.

III. 3. Sefrid Kristian M., f. 1884, g. i Am.

III. 4. Olea Johanna M., f. 1890, g. Richard Robertsen, Søberg.

III. 5. Frank Matias M., f. 1892, g. i Am.

III. 6. Andreas Berg M., 1894. Tok over farsgarden i 1919.
G. 1919 Jenny Fredrikke Robertsen, Søberg, f. 1897.
Barn:

IV. 1. Alf Martin A., f. 1920, g. 1945 Erna Helene Larsen, f. i Sørfolla 1925.
Tok over Sletten, 39/32, i 1950.
Barn: 1. Villy, 2. Anne Lovise.

John Johannessen.

IV. 2. Torleif A., f. 1924. Cand. filol. med laud 1951. Pedagogisk seminar. Hovudfag språk og historie. Var i Amerika 1952. Styrar for Bø komm. realskole frå 1853.

IV. 3. Harry Jan A., f. 1932.

III. 7. Normann M., f. 1902. I Oslo.

II. 3. Hammond Nikolai J., f. 1859. For til Am.

II. 4. Kristian Olai J. Søberg, f. 1861. Telegrafist, sist i Hønefoss. Har m. a. skreve «Fars fembøring Neptun».
G. 1896 Richarda Christofa Lockert, Mårsund.

II. 5. Ole Marelius J. Søberg, f. 1864. Fotograf og treskjerar på Steine.

II. 6. John Edvard J., f. 1870. For andre gongen til Am. i 1917, selte då fars-garden. Hadde mange interesser, m. a. for sang.
G. 1904 Jørgine Eriksen Eikemo, Taen i Hadsel, f. 1884.
Barn:

III. 1. Eivind Johan J., f. 1904.

III. 2. Birger Fredrik J., f. 1905.

III. 3. Rolf J., f. 1907.

III. 4. Ida Elisabet J., f. 1909.

III. 5. Egil Eikemo J., f. 1912.

Some of the Johannessen/Soberg family history in the *Bø Bygdebok,*
the register for all the communities in their part of the *Vesterålen*

PÅL SINE HØNER
NORSK FOLKEVISE

Pål si - ne hø-ner på hau-gan ut - slep - te,

hø - nen' så lett o - ver hau - ga-ne sprang.

Pål kun-ne vel på hø - nom for - ne - ma:

re - ven var u - te med rum-pa så lang.

Klukk, klukk, klukk, sa hø - na på hau-gom.

Pål han sprang og reng-de med au - gom:

«No tor' eg ik-kje ko-ma heim åt ho mor.»

Pål han gjekk seg litt lenger på haugen,
fekk han sjå reven låg på høna og gnog.
Pål han tok seg ein stein uti neven,
dugleg han då til reven slo.
Reven flaug, så rova hans riste.
Pål han gret for høna han miste;
«No tor' eg ikkje koma heim åt ho mor!»

«Hadd' eg no nebb, og hadd' eg no klør,
og visste eg berre kor revane låg,
skulle eg dei både rispe og klore
framantil nakken og bak over lår.
Skam få alle revane raude!
Gjev det var så vel at dei alle var daude,
så skull' eg trygt koma heim åt ho mor.

Ikkje kan ho verpe, og ikkje kan ho gala,
ikkje kan ho krype, og ikkje kan ho gå.
Eg får gå meg åt kverna og mala
og få att det mjølet eg miste i går.
Men pytt!» sa'n Pål, «eg er ikkje bangen,
kjeften og motet har hjelpt no så mangein,
eg tor' nok vel koma heim åt ho mor!»

Pål han kornet på kverna til å sleppe
så at det ljoma i kvar ein vegg,
så at agnene tok til å flyge,
og dei vart lange som geiteragg.
Pål han gav seg til å le og til å kneggje.
«No fekk eg like for høna og for egget,
no tor' eg trygt koma heim åt ho mor!»

208

Pål Sine Høner, a still-popular folk song that his father's group sang, was one of Ralph's favorites as a child. It tells what happened when Pål set his chickens free near where a fox lay in wait. (Reproduced from the *BARNAS STORE SANGBOK* compiled by Anne-Cath. Vestly, ©J.W. Cappelans Forlag A/S, Oslo, 1962.)

Another favorite has proven more elusive—Ralph recalled it as "*Stemme op en sång*" and remembered the singers coming in part by part (tenors, baritones, etc.), their voices blending beautifully. He thought the song had been written by King Gustav of Sweden.

Hardscratch in winter—codfishing time

About Lutefisk

For many Norwegians, lutefisk (literally, fish bathed in lye) is a treat, a reminder of family and home. For others, it is a never-quite-acquired taste.

Codfish to be used for lutefisk is first cleaned and decapitated and then hung to dry in the winter air. As it dries it becomes stiff and hard and can be stored for years without spoiling. Dried codfish is known as *stokkfisk*, or *tørrfisk*.

To be prepared as lutefisk, *stokkfisk* is soaked in a lye solution, traditionally made from birch ashes, for up to two weeks. The finished dish, boiled for eating, has little flavor of its own and a springy texture that can be intimidating to first-time lutefisk eaters. But it is an excellent source of protein and non-fattening as well, at least without the customary butter sauce.

Folk versions of the origin of lutefisk—which has been prepared in virtually the same way for hundreds of years—tend to be irreverent at best. One account, obviously a fairly modern one, has the *stokkfisk* buried near a telephone pole; when enough dogs have visited the pole, the story goes, the fish is worthy of being called lutefisk.

About Bootlegging

"You can't catch bootleggers with Sunday school teachers," an article by Ron Lautaret in *The Alaska Journal* (Vol. II, No. 1, 1981, pp. 35-46), is an interesting and detailed look at Prohibition in Alaska. Mr. Lautaret includes, with casual spelling intact, an anonymous letter to the territorial governor from a disgruntled citizen in Sitka that could almost have been describing the situation in Juneau when Ralph Soberg arrived:

Sitka, Alaska
July 23, 25
Dear Governor:
I sapose Alaska is a dry Tertortory—but its not so here. Moonshine is beeing sold here by the quistionable wimmin at 50c a drink.

The Old Pioneers can get out all hours in the night, cross the street and Tank up. Boys under 20 are geting it. The laundry keeps the stuff and Mr. Thomas, the Deputy sheriff, smells so of the stuff—Ladies have to move—when attending the show.

The Alaska Journal is no longer being published, but copies are accessible through the Alaska Historical Library, P.O. Box G, Juneau, AK 99811-0571.

Another interesting study of the era is a paper by Stephen Conn (edited by Antonia Moras) for the School of Justice at the University of Alaska, Anchorage. It quotes a passage from *Frontier Politics: Alaska's James Wickersham,* by Evangeline Atwood:

"Alaskans have known for two decades that their prohibition laws were a failure [said territorial Delegate Wickersham in 1933]. . . . They tell me I can expect the saloons back any time now in Alaska, once the repeal movement gets underway. But what of it? Better have saloons than smuggling, bootlegging, and other evils of an unpopular, unenforced law."

Access to Mr. Conn's paper, titled NO NEED OF GOLD—ALCOHOL CONTROL LAWS AND THE ALASKA NATIVE POPULATION: FROM THE RUSSIANS THROUGH THE EARLY YEARS OF STATEHOOD, is also available through the Alaska Historical Library. Evangeline

Atwood's biography of James Wickersham, published by Binford & Mort of Portland, Ore., in 1979, is out of print at this time.

Anyone interested in the technical aspects of moonshining—or "other aspects of plain living"—would do well to consult *The Foxfire Book*, edited with an introduction by Eliot Wigginton and published by Anchor Press/ Doubleday, Garden City, New York (Anchor Books edition, 1972).

Ralph Soberg included a postscript in his original *Confessions of an Alaska Bootlegger*:

In 1954, when I was general foreman for the Alaska Road Commission on the Kenai Peninsula, Ruth and I visited our daughter, Jackie, in Anchorage, where she was working at the federal courthouse as secretary to the U.S. district judge. Jackie had told us of a visiting judge from Juneau who had come to help with a backlog of cases in Anchorage. When he learned what she was being paid, she said, he had exclaimed, "The chambermaid at my hotel makes more than that!" and insisted that Jackie be given a civil service rating based on the job she was filling and not, as had apparently been the case, on the fact that she was 17 years old and a very recent business school graduate. Then, learning that her parents were coming to town, he had asked to meet us.

There was surprise all around when we walked into his chambers, for of course the "visiting judge" with the keen sense of fair play was George Folta, my prosecutor-turned-adviser from more than 20 years before. We had a long talk and some hearty laughs about the old days, and I was glad for the chance to say a sincere thank you for his early encouragement. Meanwhile, of course, Ruth was taking a second look at the supposedly respectable man she had married only a few years before.

I've always been proud that, when I married their mother, her girls "adopted" me. But when our younger daughter, Jerry, heard the full story, she looked at me sternly and said, "You're lucky you're not in jail."

I am lucky indeed.